Waltzing
with Bracey

Waltzing *with* Bracey

A LONG REACH HOME

BRENDA GILCHRIST

Bauhan Publishing
Peterborough, New Hampshire
2012

Library of Congress Cataloging-in-Publication Data

Gilchrist, Brenda.
Waltzing with Bracey : a long reach home / by Brenda Gilchrist.
    p. cm.
ISBN 978-0-87233-152-5 (alk. paper)
1. Gilchrist, Brenda. 2. Deer Isle (Me.)--Biography. 3. Women--Maine--Deer Isle--Biography. 4. Pembroke Welsh corgi--Maine--Deer Isle--Biography. 5. Human-animal relationships--Maine--Deer Isle. 6. Home--Maine--Deer Isle. 7. Deer Isle (Me.)--Social life and customs. I. Title.
F29.D3G55 2012
974.1'45--dc23
                                        2012004888

All watercolors and woodcuts are by the author.
All photos are from the author's collection, except the following:

Frontispiece: photo by Rod Cook (attempts were made to contact Rod Cook who was a tenant of the author)

p. 14: "Steamboat *North Haven* in Penobscot Bay" from the Elmer Montgomery Collection, Penobscot Marine Museum, and used by permission;

p. 32: "My House forty years on" photo by Rod Cook (attempts were made to contact Rod Cook who was a tenant of the author)

p. 39: Engraving of Charles Loring Brace from the Library of Congress

p. 68: "The Cunard-White Star liner *RMS Georgic*" from www.liners.dk

p. 175: "Marlboro College campus, where the Marlboro Music Festival is held" photo by Molly Tully

BAUHAN PUBLISHING LLC

7 MAIN STREET PETERBOROUGH NEW HAMPSHIRE 03458
603-567-4430

WWW.BAUHANPUBLISHING.COM   Printed in China

*To Bracey
who led the way
and Gabi
who gallantly followed in his footsteps
and whose spirits and images are intertwined*

CONTENTS

FAMILY CAST OF CHARACTERS

Charles Loring Brace—my great-grandfather

Letitia Neill Brace—my great-grandmother

Emma Donaldson, nèe Brace—my great-aunt, also known as Auntie Emma

Leta Croswell, nèe Brace—my great-aunt, also known as Auntie Leta, married to

James G. Croswell—my great-uncle, also know as Uncle Jim

Alexander Wadsworth Longfellow—cousin of Uncle Jim, also known as Waddy

Charles Loring Brace II—my grandfather

Louisa Warner Brace—my grandmother

Robert N. Brace—my great-uncle, Charles Loring's brother

Dorothy Donaldson, nèe Brace—my aunt, married to

John C. Donaldson—my uncle

Eleanor Brace—my aunt

Gerald Warner Brace—my uncle

Elizabeth Gilchrist, nèe Brace—my mother, also known as Betty or Mummie

Huntington Gilchrist—my father, also known as Dad or Daddy

John H. Gilchrist—my brother, also known as Johnnie

C. Loring Gilchrist—my brother

PROLOGUE

"She left the summer cottage to you," says my aunt's lawyer, Mr. Soule, at the other end of the line. His soft Maine tones compete with the boom boxes across the street—where the kids gather outside the monolithic Joan of Arc high school—each blaring a different song. I can hardly hear him.

"Oh, I've never *owned* a house," I stutter. Anguished over my aunt's death a few days ago, I'm near tears. "But maybe you'll tell me how to manage."

I'm not up to running a house, to carrying on family traditions. I'm a freak, a foreigner. My life in New York is work, travel, concerts and opera, and, currently, a love affair. Forty-eight years old, I'm a city girl. It's 1977.

"Well, she was fond of you," says Mr. Soule, "and certainly believed you could take care of it." I'd known for some time, in fact, that she planned to leave me the old family house. I just hadn't ever given it much thought. I loved her and didn't want her to die.

"I don't know," I say. "It's all too much. . . . I hope I can."

"Why don't you start by calling Oliver Chase," Mr. Soule says before letting me go. Chase was my aunt's caretaker and contractor.

Ill for a long time, my aunt Eleanor Brace died in a nursing home on the mainland, not far from her house on Deer Isle, off the coast of Maine. Crusty, independent New Englander that she was (if originally from New York), she hadn't wanted anyone to witness the progress of her cancer. And so, aside from her old friend Kathe Wilckins, nobody was allowed to see her.

Last summer, when I visited her, she mostly lay on the sofa in the living room, gazing out at the Camden Hills across Penobscot Bay. On a table beside her were books by and about her hero, Franklin D. Roosevelt, including several by Arthur Schlesinger. I brought her cups of tea. "Not oolong, for heaven's sake," she said. "English breakfast!"

As she leafed through the books, my aunt read aloud to me smart things Roosevelt had said. She was sharp herself, sharp as the rocks jutting out off her beach at low tide, the very ones you could smash a boat on, if you weren't careful, sailing offshore at high tide, when the rocks are hidden. She always gave me keen advice, didn't countenance foolishness. She'd taught me to sail and when and why to scrape the bottoms of dinghies.

A little late for work now, I lace up my sneakers in the minuscule front hall of my apartment on the Upper West Side of Manhattan. I'm fortunate in that I can walk to work every day through Central Park. The alders and beeches will be leafing out at last, this warm June morning.

Wearing my black, linen pants suit, I make my way on the scenic path around the southern loop of the Central Park Reservoir. I carry my low, square-heeled shoes in a tote bag; I'll change into them after I arrive at work. Beryl-gray wavelets gleam in the early morning sun as I walk, and twenty or so gulls cluster on grizzled outcroppings along the reservoir's sculpted rock edge, vaguely reminding me of the granite shoreline of Deer Isle. West and east, rows of grand, pre-war apartment buildings border the park. At the south end stands the Plaza Hotel, and, further downtown, skyscrapers re-shape the horizon to their own design. Joggled by urban walkers and runners, I walk at a fast clip under boughs of oak and elm.

On the bridle path a few feet below and parallel to the track I'm on, collies and goldens, fox terriers and poodles bound excitedly, chasing balls. Mulling over my new situation, I realize there's no way I can own a house. I can barely afford my rent-controlled apartment with its 1940s gas stove and fridge.

I exit the park onto Fifth Avenue at Ninety-first Street, and enter the Carnegie Mansion, home of the Cooper-Hewitt Museum. My job, as general editor, is to put together for the museum a series of twelve books entitled The Smithsonian Illustrated Library of Antiques, co-published by the Book-of-the-Month Club. "They need to sell at least 100,000 copies each," the director stated at my job interview. "Makes a ton of money for the museum."

I've had the job for a year now. Searching out the most distinguished scholars in their fields to write the books, I've sniffed and poked around what seems like every museum and university in the country—wining and dining directors, curators, and professors (all the while being advised that I'm on a strict budget).

"You'll have another martini, won't you?" I said invitingly the other day, ready to splurge on the director of a prestigious museum over lunch at the Carlyle. We were examining the menu, trying to decide between shad roe *en papillotte* and *filets de sole bonne femme*. I signaled the waiter, enjoying the moment.

"Okay, I'll sign up," he said. "On condition . . . "

And so we discussed terms over the filets, and then a tantalizing *tarte au citron* to close the deal, with tiny cups of espresso.

I've learned by now how to play these scenes, to appear at ease in the heady heights of the New York art world. If the art luminaries only knew how anxious I always feel as I down my martinis.

I could use one right this minute, I think to myself, circling back to the notion of owning a large summerhouse. How can I—single, with no experience of holding property, let alone property perched on a windswept, isolated island, and with no money beyond my modest publishing salary—take possession of this house? And yet, what is the alternative?

It's always been an anchor, of sorts, throughout my rootless life. But it's big, old, and reeks of history, custom, forebears. Ministers, teachers, authors, social reformers, they were long on summers and pedigree, short on money. Do-gooders, disciplinarians, sailors, dog lovers, their photographs and books and meticulously rigged ship models dominate the living room.

HOW ENGLISH YOU SOUND

The summer I was eight, my parents and I crossed the Atlantic by liner from Southampton to New York City, then traveled by steam-engine train to Rockland, Maine. From there, we came by the steamboat *North Haven* across Penobscot Bay via North Haven to Deer Isle. On a sunny July morning, we stood on the forward deck as the boat chugged out of Rockland harbor into the wide, island-filled bay. The chill breeze blew hard on my cheeks. Gulls flashed overhead in the soft-gold sunlight.

"Look at the porpoises!" I exclaimed. Their pearly bodies tunneled and veered alongside the steamboat, cavorting. My parents and I leaned over the railing for a better view.

"They're *dancing*," my mother said. She drew her long, shawl-like sweater closer around her.

"Just like my little girl in school," my father said, caressing my arm, his friendly, open face lit by the bright seas.

Not used to being alone with my parents—although my two brothers, Johnnie and Loring, eight and four years older, respectively, were almost always away at school in either the U.S. or England—I was entranced, but timorous. My governess, Miss Middleton, had stayed home in England. She was my rock.

The smell of buttery dough rose up through the vents on deck.

"Can I have pancakes for breakfast?" I asked.

"May I?" my mother corrected me gently.

My father, in tweed plus fours, led the way below to the dining room.

Families with large numbers of children sat at the tables. We ate blueberry pancakes. I poured sweet maple syrup on the puffy,

Steamboat *North Haven* in Penobscot Bay

speckled cakes and looked out the windows at passing islands, some with lighthouses and farmhouses, most with dense coverings of trees.

"The trees on the islands look like dolls' hair," I said.

"What a clever thought," my mother said. She brushed a strand of her own lustrous, almost black hair, cut fashionably short at the nape, from her right temple. Her nose was long and straight.

"But I don't suppose the islands really have faces," she said, running her fingers lightly across my forehead. Lifting her hand, she shaded her eyes against the blaze on the water.

After breakfast, we went back up to the forward deck to witness the approach to Stonington, a fishing village on the south end of Deer Isle where we would disembark.

"Put on your gloves, dear," my mother said.

The *North Haven* blasted her piercing whistle as we entered the harbor. The sound bounced off the quarries, boat sheds, fishing and lobster boats, and the white clapboard buildings that climbed straight up the steep streets on the granite hills, one above the other.

As a child, I visited Deer Isle every other summer from England, where I was born. This was my fourth trip. Johnnie was already in school in the U.S. and had a summer job, while Loring, who had crossed the Atlantic earlier, chaperoned by a family friend, was at camp.

"There's Aunt Eleanor and Ronnie!" I said, pointing at the small figure of a woman standing on the dock, with a square, black Scottie plunked beside her.

"Yoo-hoo!" Eleanor cried as the ship drew closer, waving a red kerchief for us to spot. Still slim, she had a fine figure; permed hair, reddish going on

Ronnie on the loggia

gray; aquiline, patrician profile; good bones. Her cry of greeting barely rose above the din of the ship's maneuvers alongside the wharf and the flinging of hawsers from deck to pier.

Every time we docked in Stonington, I was excited by the loud, clanking noises of the freight being unloaded and the shouts of the crew and by the salty, fishy, familiar smells—by the whole idea of landing on an island.

We climbed down to the lower deck, and my mother took my hand as we descended the gangplank, clattering beneath our steps, to the wharf, where Eleanor gave us warm, if reserved, hugs of welcome. Bending down, she lowered her fine, angular profile to my level and gave my cheek a pinch. All the while, Ronnie jumped up and down, batting his stiff brush of a tail against my calves, his paws scrabbling at my skirt and stockings.

"Glorious day, splendid trip," my father said, smiling. "What a view, with the Camden Hills, Cadillac Mountain, Isle au Haut! Always reminds me of Japan or Norway." He took off his soft cap and reached forward to give Eleanor's hand a genial shake.

A dockhand helped my father load our three large duffel bags and various carry-alls and golf clubs into Eleanor's Ford. She drove

Family house on Deer Isle

us the eight miles north, over dirt roads with views of forested inlets and far-off mountains rimming the bay, all the way to the family house on the western shore.

Viewed from the top of the driveway, I always thought the low, angular house resembled a crouched tiger gathering itself to leap out at us from its forest redoubt. As we got closer, though, the house softened, became more of a housecat, sprawled out among the rhododendrons and mountain laurel and the surrounding beds of lupine and foxglove and snapdragon.

My grandmother, Louisa Brace, and Aunt Dorothy, my mother's oldest sister, along with her husband, Uncle John Donaldson, were assembled on the vine-covered, recessed porch at the south end of the house to greet us. Their figures appeared large and shadowy against the glimmering water beyond, where distant islands, transparent in the sunlight, seemed to vanish right into the surface of the bay.

"How English you sound," my grandmother said, enfolding me in a lavender-scented embrace, even as Dorothy floated, birdlike and uncertain, amidst the confusion of hugs and exclamations of welcome.

"Yes, what a pretty accent," Dorothy said, when it was her turn to greet me, offering me a gossamer kiss on the cheek.

Meanwhile, my kindly, professorial Uncle John, portly in vest and shirt, the cuffs of his pants draped over his shoes—rumpled city and baggy country—welcomed us with laughs and quips. "I wrote a limerick for you," he said, sitting me down in a wicker chair in front of a round, green table with crooked legs. "There once was a girl named Brenda," he began in his startlingly deep voice. "Who maneuvered like a double-ender—."

"Not now, John," Eleanor said. "Let's unload this car."

Stopping obediently, he shot me a wink. I grinned back. His tidy mustache twitched over his generous lip, his round, wire-framed spectacles glistened. And without further ado, he rose to assist my father with the luggage. A foil for the more severe members of the family, John was a pied piper for my brothers, when they visited, and my male cousins, who would be invited to make model boats with him in his shop down at the Trivet, a shoreline cabin about a hundred feet north of the big house.

"What a lot of stuff, I must say," Eleanor said. "Let's bring it up to the porch first."

I still wanted to hear John's limerick. But I remained quiet and watched Ronnie play with the crab claw he had brought up onto the porch, while, silent and wraithlike, a gentle, vacant specter, Dorothy wandered about, her plumy skirt brushing against the piles of luggage and golf clubs. John always spoke for her in his letters and in conversation. He was her mouthpiece: "Dear One and I believe the world is in a sorry state," he might say, with Dorothy standing by, ever obliging, pleased to be represented.

My father put his arm around my grandmother, who held herself erect, a little apart from the turbulent scene, a graciously decorous expression on her face. She wore a bone brooch at the throat of her cream silk blouse.

"How far you've come to visit us," she said to him. "We are so grateful."

Bored with the claw by now, Ronnie scampered back and forth among our legs, cocking his half-erect, black ears at the unfamiliar tumult and nosing the aromas of the luggage.

"I don't think you'll need your golf clubs, Huntington," Eleanor said. "We've planned sailing picnics to Crow Island and also Pickering."

Not much of a sailor, least of all in Maine, which was far too cold for his liking, my father gave an appreciative nod. But he was a golfer and generally preferred to play a game on the Island's charming, hilly course.

"Brenda, dear, find your bag," my mother said. "The one with Rosie, quick." She'd allowed me to bring Rosie, my favorite doll, from England. I ran about the porch, feeling the way I imagined Ronnie must, among all the tall bodies and gangling limbs. Dorothy had absentmindedly picked up my school satchel with Rosie, books, and crayons, and stood holding it in a trance.

In my school uniform in England at age six

"May I have my bag, please?" I said to Dorothy, who seemed almost reluctant as she handed it back to me.

"Look at your nice leather gloves," Eleanor said to me, glancing down at them as she passed by to round up the luggage. "Of course, you'll have no use for them here."

I peeled them off and put them in my satchel, which I placed on the floor. Ronnie pushed his nose into it; he yearned to play tug-of-war with the gloves. I stroked his nose.

"Betty," Eleanor said to my mother, "Why on earth do you let her wear these things in Maine?"

Comfortable at last on Deer Isle

My mother thought American clothes for children, the shapeless, sloppy skirts and dreadful, machine-made sweaters, were inferior to English, even to my brown, saggy British woolen stockings and brown school blazer. In my all-brown attire matching my flat, straight hair and uncertain eyes, I stood out, different, but dim, like Dorothy.

"She doesn't have to look like a bumpkin just because she's in America," my mother said. She tossed her aubergine scarf over the shoulder of her blue linen summer coat. Out in the middle of the bay, the sheer cliffs of Hard Head Island blazed. "I want her to learn to dress well."

Youngest of the three Brace sisters, my mother was the beauty of the family. Having summered on Deer Isle as a girl, she knew her way around boats. She had the family's icy intelligence, too. But when she married my father, she went to live in Swit-

Aunt Eleanor

zerland and England, leaving the confines of Brace certitude. Awakening to fashion, she grew to prefer stylish French pajamas and wide trousers—often a scarf tied over her blouse in a floppy, loose bow. In Geneva, she waltzed with my father at the League of Nations balls in Paris gowns.

My mother on the beach in modish French pajamas

"*You* always dress well," my mother added, well aware of the closetful of neatly tailored shirtwaist dresses Eleanor had made herself in different colors and fabrics.

"Goodness me, I never thought of it that way," Eleanor said.

Eleanor urged us toward the French doors leading into the living room. With Ronnie plodding after her, she and John lugged our duffel bags through the doors. The rest of us followed: my grandmother and

The shadowed, expansive living room

Dorothy in their graceful, calf-length dresses; my handsome father, golf bag over his shoulder; and, last of all, my mother and I, with our carryalls, watchful.

The room seemed vast, as it did every time I came to visit, smelling of well-seasoned paneling and countless wood fires. I looked around to see if anything had changed. At the far end was the brick fireplace, and in the middle, the round dining table. On the stair wall hung a copy of a full-page *New Yorker* cartoon by our neighbor Gluyas Williams, next to a faded chart of the coast of Maine from Monhegan Island to Cape Elizabeth, and a model of a sloop with black-and-red hull mounted by my brother Johnnie.

Long shelves of books, many of them written by members of the family, braced the walls of the big room. Watercolors of the family boats hung on the shadowed paneling together with shore scenes by my mother's younger brother, Gerald, who now summered with his own family in an old farmhouse a couple of miles down the shore. A three-foot-long model of a gaff-rigged Quoddy Bay carry-away boat under full sail, which Gerald had bought as a boy

Eleanor's galleon, Gerald's *Roaring Forties*
on the fireplace mantle

from a local fisherman, rode above a mahogany sideboard adorned with blue-and-white platters.

Ship models, in fact, were everywhere. Deftly crafted galleons by Eleanor, America's Cup yachts by Gerald, and rugged fishing vessels by John navigated the mantelpiece and shelves and tops of birch-bark tables, and sailed among the Morris chairs and the rattan sofa. I noticed a homespun model made from cork and spools I hadn't seen before.

"Uncle John, you made a new one," I said.

He took the boat down from the shelf and handed it to me.

"A battleship," John said. "*Idumika Kumika*."

"Did you make the name up?" I said. He gave me another wink.

I twirled the spools and gun mounts, aiming them in different directions.

"You've got the hang of it," he said, patting me on the shoulder.

At that point, Muriel, a school friend of Eleanor's, came through the pantry door. She'd been in the kitchen talking to Blanche, who cooked for the family every summer. Pretty, pert-nosed, and hunch-backed, Muriel wore a flowered pinafore apron over her long-sleeved dress. She beamed at me and pressed me to her heart.

"My little chum," she said.

A week later, my parents, as they had often done on our past trips to the U.S., left me—dumped me, really—with these Brace relatives. The golf course, beguiling as it was, would have proved too small a challenge for my father, or the family too reclusive for such a sociable man. Perhaps the family, on its part, found my father overly amiable—too good-natured to be regarded seriously, notwithstanding his work with the League of Nations in Geneva and now as managing director of an American chemical company in London. And though I stayed with the Brace family during these summers, I was fundamentally a Gilchrist, whatever Braceness there might have been obliterated by the Gilchristness.

"Where are you going?" I asked my parents, invariably anxious about being left behind.

"To visit Great-Auntie Emma and friends on Cape Cod," my mother said. "Your father prefers the warmer waters."

"When will you be back?" I held Rosie tight to my chest.

Uncle John's *Idumika Kumika*

All hands scraping the dinghy

"In a while, dear," she said. She leaned down and kissed the top of my head.

The day after my parents left Deer Isle, Eleanor announced, "I plan to scrape and paint the dinghy this morning. Brenda, would you like to help me?" I'd never been invited to do this before.

"Yes!" I said.

We took the steep wooden steps down to the beach, Ronnie barreling along just ahead of us. Twisted black spruce clung to the side of the bank, reaching out into a sea that dazzled our eyes.

"Take off your stockings," she said, suddenly noticing them. "You don't need them here. I don't understand why your mother brings them."

I hung the stockings on the tall outhaul rock, around which the line to haul the dinghy was looped. Walking back over the seaweed-covered rocks, I enjoyed the crunchy slither under my bare feet. I slipped and fell at one point, misgauging the placement of rocks beneath the seaweed, which popped under my sudden weight. Ronnie nudged my ears and nose, now down at his level,

Back at the moorings

and I laughed with delight. Above us, a thin trail of fleecy white clouds divided the sky.

Eleanor wore a straw hat, a light green shirtwaist dress with a pattern of pale roses, and old tennis shoes she'd saved for wading in salt water.

We hauled the dinghy in and carried her to the top of the pebbly beach, where we proceeded to turn her over. There, Eleanor handed me a metal scraper. I began to scratch away at the green paint on the dinghy's bottom as hard as I could. A few stiff flakes fluttered off.

Eleanor held her scraper up. "Here—hold it like this," she said. "At an angle."

She gripped the back of my hand and we scraped together for a while. Finally, I continued alone on one side of the boat, scattering showers of green shavings on the pebbles around me, while she worked on the other.

"Good," Eleanor said.

Throughout my visit, my grandmother read Sir Walter Scott to me in the garden, among the peonies and tea roses, or out on the loggia, the long porch facing the bay. Our readings were formal, according to a schedule.

"My dear, we will meet on the porch," she said one clear southwesterly day. "Before lunch, at 11:30."

We sat upright on caned chairs under a green-and-white striped awning. White caps spread across the bay, struck the shore below, punched and smacked the rocks.

She put her hand over mine as she came to a particularly frightening passage of *Ivanhoe*, reading on in her temperate but exacting voice. Her long fingers tightened as Norman and Saxon knights battled to the death. "'To the battlements then,' said De Bracy; 'when didst thou ever see me the graver for the thoughts of battle? Call the Templar yonder, and let him fight but half so well for his life as he has done for his Order. . . .'"

She let the words roll and linger on her tongue, enunciating them to underscore the menacing tones. I felt privileged in her company, and timid.

A couple of days following my parents' departure, my grandmother, who had never so much as boiled an egg herself, consulted with Blanche after lunch about the menu that night. Independent, spirited, Blanche was descended from an old Island settlers' family.

"We'll have lobster stew, dear Blanche, if Fifield's has any lobsters," my grandmother said. "And your delicious blancmange for dessert." Blanche made it with the white, frilly seaweed we picked up on our shore.

"There's no lobsters I know of at Fifield's today," Blanche responded. "How 'bout a nice haddock chowder?" Haddock it would be.

"We came home wing on wing from one of the Porcupine islands this afternoon," Eleanor said at the dining table that evening, as she shook out her linen napkin and placed it in her lap. "Made good headway."

Every evening at supper there would be endless analyses of dealings with virulent tides and currents and challenges of gales and fog. Discussions of the finer points of rigging and navigation could dominate an entire meal. "The grommet in the *Forties'* mains'l is loose," Eleanor had said to John two nights before, the first evening on my own with the family.

"I'll fix it at the clew tomorrow," John said.

"Good. It'll make it easier to fetch to windward."

"Or box off," John said, merrily, as he snared a scallop with his fork.

I longed to say something, but had neither the courage nor the expertise.

After we finished the chowder, I watched my grandmother pull a tiny silver anchor hanging from the ceiling on a string at eye level. The string was tied to the end of a wire that threaded its way across the ceiling to the kitchen, where it rang a bell.

Blanche opened the door from the kitchen. "Do you want dessert?" she asked. My grandmother nodded. Blanche disappeared, only to return carrying the blancmange, quivering and shimmering, on a platter to the table.

Supper over, the family helped clear the dishes. John took charge in the kitchen as chief bottlewasher. For all his kindliness, I wasn't often in his company, and so it was an honor to be included in this nightly rite. He arranged two pots side by side in the sink—one for washing, one for rinsing—and filled them with water heated on the oil cookstove. First, he poured precisely one-half cup Ivory Flakes into the washing pan and frothed the flakes up. Dorothy, Eleanor, and I were handed immaculate, faded dishtowels.

"Remember, dear ones," he said. "Use light, spiral strokes for those thin green plates." Flourishing a silver knife, he described circles in the air. He might have been teaching his anatomy class at the University of Pittsburgh Medical School.

"The way you're carrying on, waving that knife, John," Eleanor said, "it's a wonder your students learn anything from you."

Later, the dishes done, we sat by the fire, reading silently by kerosene lamps. The only sounds were of the fire crackling and Ronnie snoring. My grandmother—beautiful, regal almost, in her soft, flowing, lavender two-piece knitted ensemble—sat on the rattan sofa. Sighing over her book, *The Good Earth* by Pearl Buck, she brought it up from her lap and adjusted her pince-nez on a chain. I heard her whisper the words: "'And up from the quiescent, waiting land a faint mist rose, silver as moonlight, and clung about the tree trunks.'" Her book was about China, I knew. But she glanced at me and turned to look out a window facing east, away from the water. My eyes followed hers. There, in the twilit garden, was the very same mist—transparent white, hugging the spruce trees.

Dorothy, a softer, vaguer version of my grandmother, sat on the sofa next to her, embroidering a linen handkerchief. She spent her days cutting zinnias, daylilies, and roses in the garden and arranging them in vases, which she placed throughout the house. Room to room, she wandered, snipping and shaping the bouquets, gently vacant, useless, it seemed, at any other task.

John was seated in one of the Morris chairs beside the fireplace. He coughed, sucked on his pipe, his maritime history book propped on a pillow in his lap. Eleanor, in the other Morris chair, deeply immersed in Emil Ludwig's *Roosevelt*, held her book close to the flecked white lamp, the mantle glowing like a miniature beacon. Years after, Eleanor would become a Henry A. Wallace supporter—a radical stance even in this family of Democrats. But until her dying day, her first love would always remain FDR.

My own book was *Swallows and Amazons* by Arthur Ransome, which I soaked up eagerly in my wicker chair next to Eleanor and my grandmother, homesick for England, for the moors and bogs, for the girls in the story. . . .

Eleanor tended the fire. Early in the evening, she shifted the burning pieces with an iron poker to the back and added two medium-sized spruce logs at the front on the andirons, spaced far enough apart so they didn't smoke.

Once, when I saw the fire burning down, I summoned the cour-

By the fire

age to place a small log at the front, exactly as I'd seen Eleanor do. The fire smoked, and I noticed Eleanor glance up briefly. Returning to my chair, I pretended to continue reading, my heart pounding. If only the log would catch. Should I try again? Then Eleanor rose from her chair and moved the log the slightest bit with the poker: the smoke stopped, the air cleared.

It was like sailing: you had to do it right.

John wasn't talented at fires, either, I consoled myself. *Or* at sailing, his grand passion. He was a total bumbler compared to Eleanor, who always made perfect moorings, stopped dead beside the buoy, picked it up as though it was a piece of sponge cake.

"Eleanor, dear, the fire burns beautifully," my grandmother suddenly remarked "What did you do? You always do the right thing."

As always, I felt enclosed by the circle, but separate from it. I'd never succeed at the fire, I thought; I'd never learn. And yet it was so quiet. Not a word of criticism spoken.

"May I go upstairs?" I asked. "I'd like to read in bed." My grandmother nodded.

Muriel was my refuge. At 8:30 p.m., I was allowed to have a bath and visit her. No one else in the family went upstairs before 9. But Muriel, granted leniency from the Brace rules, had already gone ahead to her room.

Though schooled in America, Muriel was English. Brits together, we giggled and confided. I could say things to her I simply couldn't to the family sitting quietly downstairs.

"Why does Grandma wear those funny glasses on a chain?"

"*Shhhh.* Don't let her hear you say that!" The walls in the house were so thin you could hear a whisper from one end to the other.

I put a pillow over my mouth to stifle my chortles, whereupon she grabbed it off and made a face by pulling her mouth wide with her fingers.

In later years, we talked about boys.

Winters, Muriel lived with Eleanor, my grandmother, and Ronnie in a spacious, antiques-filled apartment on East Seventy-second Street in New York City. When she wasn't seeing friends at the Cosmopolitan Club, a few blocks down, on Sixty-sixth Street, Muriel ran the household and looked after my grandmother, while Eleanor worked at Miss Hewitt's Classes, where she taught typing and other business skills.

In bed, Muriel read the *London Illustrated News.* Downstairs you weren't supposed to read magazines, only edifying literature—the Bible, of course, and religious books; European, maritime, and political histories; Greek and English poetry. Novelists like Angela Thirkell, Sir Walter Scott, and Anthony Trollope were acceptable. The rules were frequently flouted, however. This evening, after all, Eleanor had chosen her popular FDR book, and Grandma, her bestseller by Pearl Buck.

You could keep what you liked in your bedroom. I had Nancy Drew; Eleanor, murders; John, naval thrillers. Grandma usually got into bed and fell right to sleep. I assumed Dorothy, who wasn't much of a reader, did also.

My room, at the back of the house, formerly a maid's room,

The big spruce trees around the house

faced the woods. Through the open window, I could smell spruce and pine on the cool salt air. I cuddled Rosie on the pillow beside me and watched the moon rise above the trees and float in a misty cloud across the navy blue sky.

"My" house, forty years on

→ 2 ←

THE DANGEROUS CLASSES

On a windy July day forty years on, I drive down toward my aunt's—*my*—house on Deer Isle for the first time since inheriting it. The house gives the illusion, from a distance, of being engulfed by waves—a ship foundering at sea. Quite different from the image of the tiger I entertained as a child. Breakers appear to crash right up on the porch, though, of course, they're actually a hundred feet beyond, too far to do damage. Pummeling the rocks down on the beach with true, foamy fury, they send spray over the tall bank and onto the rough grass and juniper between the house and shore.

At the foot of the circle driveway, I park my rented car and step onto the porch. Tasting mist from the spray on my lips, I notice tiny droplets on the caned seats of the steamer chairs, which Oliver Chase must have placed here.

It's quiet, except for the squealing and whining of gulls, the cawing of crows, and the din of waves. No one urges me to unload the car or comments on my accent or calls me chum. No dog runs around with a crab claw. I carry my suitcase and a box of books from the car to the porch. The chairs, arranged to face the view, remain damp and empty.

Standing there, I gaze at the familiar islands: Bradbury with its tight capping of spruce; Butter, its ocherous meadow; Hard Head, its freshet of surf.

Apprehensive, scared of facing my responsibilities, my ghosts, I'm poised to cross an ocean of avoidance. I remind myself how many times I've been to this house, how many times I've rolled about in the Atlantic between two lives. Beached on this shore as a child, I regarded the house as a kind of haven, if never really a home.

I walk around the house before entering it, thinking how very well Alexander Wadsworth Longfellow designed the low-slung profile to blend into the surroundings. The weathering of shingles and green paint on the trim since it was built in 1902 have helped the house almost disappear into the Down East mix of tall, taper-

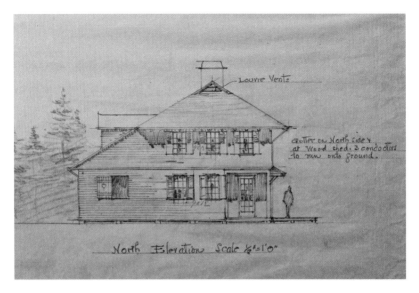

Longfellow's drawing of the north side

ing white spruce, taller red spruce, and the smattering of Eastern hemlock and Norway spruce. The great, original porch we called the loggia, running the length of the side of the house facing the water, long ago rotted away, and Eleanor had it taken down. Only a stoop remains. What a project it will be to put it back, I think—totally out of line to consider such a possibility, a voice inside me says.

Waddy, as Henry's nephew was known, was a successful architect. In Maine alone he had numerous commissions from moneyed clients to build sizable "cottages" in Bar Harbor and Northeast Harbor. When he designed the innovative, shingle-style cottage on

Deer Isle for his cousin, my great-uncle, James Greenleaf Croswell, who was also a nephew of the poet, I suspect he was doing him something of a favor. My great-uncle, whom everybody in the family affectionately called Uncle Jim, was headmaster of the Brearley School for Girls in New York City, where my mother went while he was head, and which I attended long after he died. He set a scholarly tone at the school that continues to this day. Greek scholar

Auntie Leta and Uncle Jim

(he'd taught at Harvard, too), early feminist, and idol of teachers, he was of uncommon erudition but comparatively modest means. Described as the "nicest man who ever lived" by my Uncle Gerald, Uncle Jim, who married my great-aunt Leta Brace, my grandfather's sister, was a benign presence in the family. His ghost accompanies me as I stroll beside the beds of old-fashioned day lilies surrounding the house and the clumps of rosa rugosa.

On my return to the porch, I enter the umbrageous, expansive living room through the French doors. Momentarily petrified—I feel as though I'm twelve, not almost fifty—I pause in the doorway. Who am I to traverse this threshold into the sacred family precinct? I look for Ronnie, wishing to drop down to snuffle his fragrant, fishy, damp coat.

The familiar aroma of pine paneling and fir floor calms me somewhat, and I fetch my suitcase and box from the porch, placing them firmly, with the suggestion of a thud, on the living room floor. I square my shoulders and face the room: the big round dining table, moved to the bay window added by Eleanor; the fireplace with the Morris chairs on either side; the ship models everywhere; and the long rows of my forebears' books, stationed like silent sentinels along the dusky walls.

Remember, I tell myself, I'm an editor in New York. I handle eminent authors and their books all the time. It's my job. Not to say I don't continually worry I'm not smart enough or creative enough or chic enough to cope with the task and to move in such rarefied circles.

So, yes, my great-grandfather Charles Loring Brace's notable religious and social tomes—with titles such as *The Dangerous Classes of New York*, *Gesta Christi*, and *The Unknown God*—intimidate me. His presence looms over the room, darkens it with weighty piety. His good works infiltrate the house. I feel excluded, a stranger.

I have an entry visa, I want to shout: a safe-conduct pass, clearance papers from Eleanor. I am the owner of this house!

Surely, I can learn to talk to contractors, electricians, plumbers, and wood stackers as competently as I do to designers, production directors, and sales managers. I can learn to discuss the replacement of shingles and reinforcement of foundation posts as capably as I do the quality and heft of spines and bindings. I learned French twice, after all. I've lived in and traveled to England, France, Belgium, Holland, Pakistan, and India—you name it. My experience is wide, you could say.

Unpersuaded, my mind goes silent, and I sit at the dining table, watch a hummingbird at the vine outside the window sip and dart among the honeysuckle blossoms. I notice the old, weight-driven, wooden shelf clock on the mantelpiece, with its reverse-painted scene of Buckingham Palace on the door's glass pane. I insert the key into the ancient face and wind it three times. With my index finger, I move the hands into place and swing the pendulum. The clock begins to tick tock, the measured, staccato sound filling the room.

Gathering strength, I make my way to the kitchen, through the pantry, whose shelves (more shelves!) are piled with old china, including twelve ornate Royal Munich porcelain plates, each decorated with a different kind of bird, a partridge or mallard, and a set of English Princess Rose tea ware. I stow the few provisions I picked up en route and put together a tuna fish sandwich for lunch.

Afterward, I carry my bag upstairs, where there are four large bedrooms, plus the former maid's room I slept in as a child. I choose, with a certain amount of trepidation, to sleep in Eleanor's room, which has a triple exposure at the southern end.

Back downstairs, I remove copies of my great-grandfather's books from the shelves. I rub my thumb across the deep blue and burgundy cloth bindings, riffle through the heavy, yellowing pages. Gilt letters glow dully on the covers, and puffs of musty odors emanate, along with edifying thoughts.

As I examine these books, I think of my job at the Cooper-Hewitt, where I not only sign up authors but help plan the format and scope of the lavishly illustrated volumes for the Smithsonian series. I consult museum curators, professors, and collectors on whether to have separate books on porcelain and pottery, whole volumes on silver or clocks. I hire a designer, photographers, and editors.

It's an ambitious undertaking by the museum, which only recently became part of the Smithsonian and hopes to turn a profit with the books. (My first mission was a scary, exploratory trip to Washington, D.C., to ask for the Smithsonian's cooperation. "Your museum has some audacity using our name in this endeavor," a curator at one of the Smithsonian museums yelled at me, slamming his department door in my face. "You only just became a *part* of the Smithsonian!")

I have a small budget. "Don't offer the authors royalties," the Cooper-Hewitt director told me. "Only fees."

"But I'm contacting the best scholars in the field!" I protested.

The Book-of-the-Month Club, co-publisher of the series, fed up with the museum's stinginess, decided one day to move me physically to their own offices in midtown. They sent a truck uptown and loaded all my office paraphernalia—and me—into it; we left my assistant at the museum as a spy. Relieved and flattered at first, I was also unnerved. Surely the editors at the BOMC would see through and expose me as a fraud.

"Doesn't the museum understand you have to spend money to make money?" the managing editor at the BOMC confided to me, with frustration.

Although the BOMC is my protector, I still need to fight occasionally for money. "We can't afford the peacock-blue linen for the binding," the director of the production department said to me last week, his face barely visible above the heights of galleys, mechanicals, blues, and repros on the conference table between us. "Too pricey."

"But it's soooo sumptuous," I tried, fingering an elegantly nubbled sample. Summoning my courage, I added, "Anyway, your own sales department agrees with the Cooper-Hewitt Museum that we can sell a hundred thousand copies of each volume . . ."

I recall the scene as I stand in front of the bookshelves in the Deer Isle living room. I convey a copy of *Life and Letters of Charles Loring Brace*, bound in brown linen, edited by my great-aunt, his daughter Emma Brace, to the rattan sofa where my grandmother read and Dorothy darned socks by the fire. Published in 1894, a quarter century after Brace's first book, it has wider margins and a less pungent smell than the earlier volumes. A formidable person herself, Auntie Emma, on her occasional visits to Deer Isle, would say, as the family sat down for supper, "I will not tolerate talk about sailing at this table, only consequential issues of the day."

Through the bay window, I see a couple of crows stalk the grass beside the driveway. Gusts of a crisp southwesterly enter the room through the porch door, cooling my neck and shoulders as I read one of his letters to a friend dated 1866:

Charles Loring Brace

> Probably few human beings ever had a more real sense of things unseen than I habitually have. The eternal and the infinite are sometimes so near to me that all life seems insignificant, and I watch the steady revolution of days bearing me toward the vast mystery as steadily as we count the days on a sea-voyage before reaching home; and yet there are certain influences of a very petty kind which can temporarily close up the heavens to me, and shut me up in a very narrow cell, and can veil the face of the unseen Father.

Here the Great Man descends from overfleshed arrogance to adamant self-abnegation in two sentences! A pompous guy? Yes, but with his own fiends, apparently. Perhaps he's human after all. I certainly identify with the "very narrow cell."

I turn to the shelves again and select his *Dangerous Classes: Twenty Years of Work Among Them.* Published in 1873, it became a classic in its field. I receive a sour whiff from its pages:

> In the view of this book, the class of a large city most dangerous to its property, its morals and its political life, are the ignorant, desti-

tute, untrained, and abandoned youth: the outcast street-children grown up to be voters, to be the implements of demagogues, the "feeders" of the criminals, and the sources of domestic outbreaks and violations of law.

The old clock ticks solemnly on the mantelpiece.

I leaf further through the book:

Their life was, of course, a painfully hard one. To sleep in boxes, or under stairways, or in hay barges on the coldest winter-nights, for a mere child, was hard enough; but often to have no food, to be kicked and cuffed by the older ruffians, and shoved about by the police, standing barefooted and in rags under doorways as the winter-storm raged, and to know that in all the great city there was not a single door open with welcome to the little rover—this was harder.

Human after all! But this, of course, was his great passion, to save poor children. It's what he was known for.

"Yet, with all this," he goes on to write. "a more light-hearted youngster than the street-boy is not to be found. He is always ready to make fun of his sufferings, and to 'chaff' others."

He loves them!

Growing up summers in this house, I heard all about how my great-grandfather was a friend of Charles Darwin and John Stuart Mill; how he founded the Children's Aid Society in New York City in 1853 and conceived of the Orphan Trains, which eventually rescued as many as two hundred fifty thousand homeless children from the streets of New York; and how he influenced his childhood friend Frederick Law Olmsted (who also summered on Deer Isle toward the end of his life) to design parks for the poor as well as the wealthy and, additionally, converted him to abolitionism.

Although Brace's impact on the world of social welfare was doubtless important—he was, and still may be, the pre-eminent figure in American child welfare history—it has had mixed results in our family. My grandfather Charles Loring Brace II., carried on his work with devotion, if dutifully. But in our efforts to live up to the great man's touted rectitude—whether we understood or were aware of what we were doing or not—many of us have been brought to our knees. I took only a minimum interest in his career in my youth, but his influence is in the marrow of the family's bones, and has seeped into the house, shadowing the walls, and burdening the psyche. Failure and confusion joined to self-defeating ancestor worship and grandiosity have taken their toll. Alcoholism is not an uncommon disease in any family so freighted. My brother Loring, a talented writer, died of the disease in his early fifties. Its wings have brushed me, too.

Over the following days, between unpacking and adjusting to my unfamiliar, new role as Down East chatelaine, I pursue my odyssey through the bookshelves. The next morning, after finishing breakfast at the big green table in the bay window, I glance at Harriet Beecher Stowe's novel *Oldtown Folks*, full of pseudonymous Braces (identified by my uncle Gerald on the flyleaf). But I discover I'm tired of these eminences.

I'll deal with Harriet another time, I decide.

A couple of hours later, I drive to the village of Deer Isle to shop at the grocery store and say hello to Donna at the checkout counter. "So, Eleanor died, did she?" Donna said. "Nice lady, she was. Always liked her."

Back at the house, I scan Gerald's own shelf of books (I can't stop, despite my resolutions), including his best-selling novel *The Garretson Chronicle* and his most successful work of nonfiction, *Between Wind and Water*. I've read almost all his books.

The wind increases a notch. Clouds thicken over the Camden Hills. Not yet comfortable in this vexatious house, I reach up to a high shelf to search for more sympathetic characters among the leather-bound photograph albums piled there. I find a photograph of Grandma Louisa and her sister-in-law, Great-Auntie Leta, Uncle Jim's wife, wearing long white dresses with tucked sleeves, standing among the same steamer and Adirondack chairs that are still in use on the verandah. Leta holds a tabby cat; she and my grandmother are laughing. In another photo, my grandfather and assorted great-uncles,

Auntie Leta, right, on porch with family

including Uncle Jim, with pipes in their mouths and wearing white shirts and bowties, lounge on a grassy promontory by the water among the remains of their picnic—empty lobster pails, scattered plates, picnic basket. Another photo, taken on the same promontory, shows Uncle Jim reading a volume of what must be, given his proclivities, Greek poetry.

A framed print of the picnic scene also hangs in the master bedroom upstairs, along with a photograph of my Irish great-grandmother, Letitia. Lace cap on her head, knitted shawl over her silk brocade dress with white cuffs, she's sternly bent over her crochet

Grandfather Charles Loring Brace II; Great-uncle James Croswell; Great-uncle Robert N. Brace

hook. Her father, Robert Neill, was an active abolitionist in Belfast in the 1850s—in fact, Frederick Douglass visited him. There I go again . . . I can't help being impressed by these people, yet they suffocate me.

In the center of the living room, I turn slowly to view the water-colors and ship models

Uncle Jim reading Greek poetry

made by family members. Eleanor's geometric hooked rugs float on the worn, deep brown fir floor. English "Paradise" dessert plates, French porcelain teapots, and Export platters adorn the sideboard.

I once asked Eleanor, "Have you read Great-grandfather's books?"

"Well, of course not," she'd said. "But I've read all of Uncle Jim's letters."

I'm comforted to discover Uncle Jim's volume of witty and original letters to friends and family, *Letters and Writings of James Greenleaf Croswell*, among them his young nieces Eleanor and Betty (my mother), and other writings on a corner shelf by the fireplace.

I carry the book to a steamer chair on the loggia and sniff the briny atmosphere. Away from the noiseless utterances in the living room, the intonings against the evils of poverty, I read a letter he wrote to Eleanor from Somerset, England, where he and Auntie Leta and her sister, my great-aunt Emma, had gone on a trip: The letter is dated 1896, when Eleanor would have been seven.

> We live in a cottage. There is a duck-pond in front. The little ducks swim in the pond. Little boys throw sticks at the little ducks. The ducks say Quack! quack! Good Aunt Croswell says "Get out, little

boy!" Good Aunt Emma says "Little boy! How would you like to have sticks thrown at you." He goes away. Tomorrow we shall eat one of these ducks. Aunt Croswell will have two pieces and Aunt Emma one piece. Dear little ducks! I think we shall not eat them. "They are too pretty," says Good Aunt Croswell. "We will eat potatoes and gooseberries which are very good but not pretty." Binkle [Uncle Jim's nickname] is good but not pretty. Do people eat those who are good, but not pretty? Would you eat Binkle? Or a pretty duck?

I have to love this guy. A raft of eiders drifts by, and I start to feel a bit more comfortable. Perhaps Uncle Jim sat in this very same chair and admired the ducks off this shore.

My grandmother always read to me out on the old loggia. So many memories of books. Is this why I ended up in publishing, I wonder?

Stretching my legs on the footrest, I browse through the book and find a letter from Uncle Jim to my mother—she would have been seventeen and Eleanor twenty-four—dated 1913 from Deer Isle:

August 8 a picnic to Great Spruce Head. Very calm going out. Fog settled on us at lunch. Eleanor and I made the course, however, and sailed home in a fresh breeze (south by east). We didn't see land for three quarters of an hour, and we hit exactly on her mooring so that we only had to get in the jib and luff.

Auntie Leta was tickled to death with that trip. So was I. We did it fine. Steering by Eleanor. All our sailing is done by Eleanor. Eleanor is a dandy. I would go anywhere with her steering. She is very wise and very clever with the boat; and brings out all the boat's good qualities—and mine too. Tell your mother so. My nieces are certainly fine. They ought to have better uncles and aunts. . . . Auntie Leta sends her love to you all. She and Eleanor sleep out in tents. They never get up in the morning. Eleanor comes silently brushing in about 9, like a great moth caught by daylight.

Yes, I went everywhere with Eleanor steering. In fact, I remember thirty-five years ago almost to the day—I was thirteen and Eleanor, fifty-four—I had *exactly* the same experience with her that Uncle Jim describes.

Roaring Forties off the Point

From the porch, I watch the bay shimmer in the sunlight. The lighthouse on Eagle sparkles. I can see the tip of Great Spruce Head, discernible beyond the monumental cliffs of Hard Head.

Putting aside Uncle Jim's book, I follow the memory of my sail with Eleanor straight back to the day in August she and I set course for Eagle. Finished with our picnic and exploration of the island, we discovered—as so often happens on this part of the coast—that the wind had freshened more than we expected. This was a rare occurrence for Eleanor, however, whose success at predicting

Eleanor sailing the *Forties* under a reefed jib without the mainsail

weather was well nigh 100 percent. We came back in a howling, stiff nor'wester under a reefed jib, practically bare poles. Without the mainsail, there was no way to steer Eleanor's sixteen-foot sloop *Roaring Forties* to her mooring off Dunham's Point, no way to steer her at all, except in a straight line southeast. So with Eleanor at the helm, we ran to windward toward Sylvester's Cove. Entering the crammed harbor at breakneck speed, Eleanor hollered at me, "Drop the jib!" as we careened abreast of an unoccupied mooring in our path. She grabbed the buoy from the stern. A fabulous Bracian feat, Eleanor grinning and relaxed.

Eleanor had begun to teach me to sail that summer. She handed the tiller over to me on our sails, without fuss or heavy-duty instruction.

"You'll find out soon enough if you do something silly," she said.

Two years subsequent to my sail to Eagle with Eleanor, I made my first solo sail in July in the *Forties*, at age fifteen—pretty old for a serious sailor to be finally going it alone. "Remember, on the way home, you'll be before the wind," John said at breakfast, the morning of my solo. "When you stand for the mooring, sail close to the wind and fetch about on top of it."

John sipped his hot water (never coffee, only hot water, sometimes with a wedge of lemon) and bit into his toast. "Current's strong off the point. No leeway. If you miss, you'll pile up on the rocks," he said.

"Oh, for heaven's sake, John, you're scaring her to death," Eleanor said. She smoked a Chesterfield with her cup of black coffee.

"You'll head for the rocks,

Uncle John's *Charmian*

and, at low tide, with no room to maneuver, you'll go aground," John said. "You'll come a cropper."

He knew: he'd hit about every rock in the bay in his elegant, mahogany sloop, *Charmian*. Once, when my mother and Eleanor and I were aboard, the summer I was six, he stranded her hard and fast on a reef in the busy thoroughfare off Stonington. Eleanor rowed my mother and me in the tender to the town dock, where friends waited.

"We hit a rock!" I shouted. My mother kicked my foot, lightly. "Shhh! dear. We don't want to draw *attention* . . ."

At 10 a.m., when the wind settled into its seasonal, southwesterly pattern for the day, I went down to the beach below the house. John, in his standard Chaplinesque dress of baggy pants, red suspenders, white shirt, and ragged beige cardigan, accompanied me. He observed me pull the dinghy in on the outhaul and row out to the *Forties*.

The boat was a high-sided, wooden double-ender with a centerboard. Designed by Gerald (who designed all the family boats), she'd been built on Eagle about ten years before. She was named the *Roaring Forties*, after the prevailing winds in the South Indian Ocean (Eleanor happened to be in her forties at the time).

By mooring their boats off their own shore, rather than at the Deer Isle Yacht Club, a mile away in Sylvester's Cove, the family avoided having to socialize. For although the club had no building, only a dock, even this would have required more intercourse than the aloof, solitary Braces could tolerate. The family was not totally consistent, however. Gerald entered and won the club's annual Round the Island race in his sloop Festina one summer. And John, by far the most affable member of the family, was elected

Eleanor and *Forties* at the mooring

Forties before the wind

commodore of the club another summer.

As I climbed into the *Forties* from the dinghy, John leaned back against the outhaul rock. He took his pipe from his cardigan pocket and lit it. Eleanor, on the bluff above the beach, her straw hat bending in the breeze, followed me with her binoculars. My grandmother, in a mid-calf checked skirt, sat on the bench nearby.

"Come back before it's dead low tide," John hallooed across the water. "Or change your strategy for the mooring."

"She may have to change her strategy for other reasons," Eleanor shouted to him. Barely audible to me, her voice would have carried on a direct pitch to John, downwind of her.

In the years that followed, when John and I sailed together in the *Forties*, we'd dwell companionably on the negatives, the perils. Before leaving the mooring, we'd begin discussing the best way to catch it when we got back. Should we luff and make a big, slow circle or come at it close-hauled in a fast, savage direct hit? We analyzed the many variations, worrying each one like a dog's chew toy, in such intricate detail that we barely noticed the sail itself.

I raised the mainsail and jib, tied the dinghy to the mooring with a mandatory bowline, cast the line over the side, and backed

I sailed even in the rain

the jib. The sails filled and I headed out, perfectly alone, into the eastern bay. The boat heeled, picked up power and speed. Crotchety and bloody-minded in close quarters (she was the most difficult boat he'd ever sailed, Gerald told me many years later, to my surprise, not long before he died), the *Forties* was comfortable and sassy out in open water.

Far from the shore, far from my watching relatives, intoxicated with the freedom, I sang Beethoven's *Eroica* at the top of my lungs.

Gulls floated in the current of air above the mast and the bow swooshed through the sea. Exhilarated, enraptured, I was in a fever of excitement. I felt like I'd been shoved out of a small plane with a parachute.

My course, which, in the brisk southwest breeze, took little more than an hour, had been set by John and Eleanor. I sailed northwest toward densely forested Bradbury, south to treeless Hard Head, inhabited only by gulls and cormorants, and east back to the point— to the mooring, where I turned on a dime, stopping dead! Perfect.

Eleanor and my grandmother applauded from the bluff, John clapped and whooped from the beach. I only wished Uncle Jim could have seen me. Would he have called me a dandy?

Would they believe me capable of taking command of this house, my older self wonders? Would they applaud me now?

Following the solo trial, in a delirium of joy, I sailed alone in the *Forties* every day. Sailing became my obsession, the only thing I wanted to do. I finally understood the family axiom that a day without a sail was a day lost. Of course, I continued to dread doing the "wrong" thing. But most of the time, the wind filled the sails exactly right. There's a correct way to do this, after all. Otherwise, you can fall off the wind, dangerously off the wind, get knocked down or sail too close to the wind, drift in the currents, canvas flapping in the middle of the bay, wasting wind.

"Brenda, you're in irons," Eleanor once said to me when, my attention having wandered, the sails fluttered and we lost our momentum out near Bradbury as the tide soon swept us backward. I recall her words now with chagrin. A cloud passes over Hard Head and casts a shadow on the high, chalky cliffs.

Back then, I became addicted to the sport. I dreamed about it every night, and actually started to join in the nautical discussions at supper.

"I returned from Pickering Island in a quartering sea this afternoon," I said proudly one evening. How I longed for Eleanor's praise. "Splendid," she said, and I helped myself to a serving of steamed clams.

"Did you yaw?" asked John mischievously.

"Of *course* not," I said, frowning. Noticed a bit, accepted for my skills, I had grown in confidence.

I gaze out on the scene of that sailing triumph of more than a quarter century earlier. Bradbury, Hard Head, and the Point still mark my course. Turning back to Uncle Jim's letters, I find another one to my mother written the same summer, when she was seventeen:

> I think you are a good deal of a dreamer. Aren't you? Well, you have a right to be. Those lovely years, sixteen to twenty-six, which you live in now, are full of dreams. Go ahead, and have a lot of dreams. I will keep as still as a mouse; and keep everybody else still, if I can. I dream myself sometimes, and I know how nice it is for little girls to dream.

⇥ 3 ⇤

FINDING BRACEY

"Go home! *Go home!*" Eleanor yelled at Ronnie, paddling furiously after us as we rowed the dinghy out to go for a sail together in the *Forties*. "You can't come!"

A brisk westerly blew across the bay that late July morning, a couple of weeks after my first solo sail.

Ronnie's cloddy body continued to barrel through the water.

"You'll get tangled in the jib sheet," she cried at him over the dinghy's frothy wake, "hang yourself on the hawser."

But he knew precisely how far he'd have to swim before she'd give in and haul him over the gunwale into the pram. Unrepentant, he'd shake himself, spraying cold salt water on our shirts and pants, misting our sunglasses.

In fact, Ronnie was a rather good sailor, remaining squarely amidships, whether the boat pinched or heeled. And when Eleanor cried, "Ready about, hard alee," he'd flatten himself astern. He was a model crew, a fine example to me.

Several years pass, and I'm picnicking on the rocky beach below the house in June with Clint and Varney, up visiting from Massachusetts. Varney and I are old friends from New York. It's been nine years since Eleanor died, but I haven't been able to use the house much. I can't afford to. I rent it out mostly, coming in June to open it and again in September to close it. A bit of a burden, this routine, but I can't give up the house. The family ghosts are too powerful.

I still live and work in New York. The Smithsonian series wrapped up successfully five years back, in 1981. We managed to produce twelve handsome, informative, saleable volumes in the course of the project—and to sell the desired number of copies. Two months after my job ended, I drove to Maine to take care of my mother, who had been ill with breast cancer for several years. I'd flown to Portland periodically to visit her in the hospital there or at her home in Wiscasset. But I hadn't been free to spend much time with her.

She died the morning after I arrived that last visit, as I sat by her bedside, holding her hand. Devastated, I walked for hours along the streets of Wiscasset, past white houses with columns and widows' walks and Palladian windows, unable to stop crying, the tears flowing down my cheeks, utterly lost, though grateful I'd been there, able to embrace her—a gentle, quiet scene, the feeling of closeness unusual for us, a calm goodbye.

My mother left me a little money, enough so that, were I to patch it together with my freelance income, I might some day be able to live in the house on Deer Isle year round, if I chose to. And so I decided not to take on a permanent job, though I had offers, instead freelancing for the Metropolitan, the Guggenheim, and the Princeton Art Museum, among other institutions, editing scholarly festschrifts and catalogs.

On the beach, Varney and Clint and I prop our backs against the large boulder formerly used for the outhaul, the water offshore now without a mooring. Varney pours iced tea from a thermos into three paper cups decorated with blueberries.

"I need a buddy," I ruminate out loud, offering my friends crab-meat rolls and coleslaw, "a palsy-walsy to help me decide what to do with the house, with my life. A partner."

"What you need is a dog!" Varney cries. "Who follows his nose!"

"Well, I don't know," I say. "I've never actually owned a dog of my very own." Though I recall our family dogs with affection: Gillie, a perky, small Scottie; and Piers, a sober, sweet-hearted cocker spaniel.

"You need to learn to run free," Clint agrees, waving his fork and inadvertently scattering coleslaw on the stones. "Like that boat out there!" He points to an O'Day Sailer running by before the wind.

The next day, on a trip to the hardware store to buy a Phillips head screwdriver, I see a short-legged, red and black canine with white markings stationed near a display of slip-joint and long-nose pliers.

"Such a bewitching pooch," I coo, leaning down to stroke the animal's tapered muzzle, as the owner, blond going-on gray in a taupe-and-tan peasant skirt, experiments with a pair of end-nippers.

"What kind of a dog is it?" I say.

"Corgi, Pembroke Welsh corgi—the Queen's dog," she says, fluffing the ruffled neck on her blouse.

"What a downy coat," I say, gently stroking the puppy's fur. "Where did you get it?"

"Sedgwick, across the bridge." She gives me the phone number of the breeder.

My goose is cooked, but as soon as I report back to Varney and Clint, I begin to backpedal. "It's all I can do to cope with this house and garden," I protest, as they set their bags down in the front hall to say goodbye.

"A dog will *help* you!" Varney urges.

"And how is it going to live in New York?" I say

"It will meet tons of dogs," Clint says, patting my arm.

"Call the breeder," Varney says, with loving sternness as the screen door knocks against her heel. "You're on your own."

"A dog as well as a house?" I call out after them as they drive away. But maybe they're right. Maybe one burden, in effect, eases another. Not that I have time to do anything before I return to New York. The big house must be cleaned and the windows washed. I weed the flowerbeds and plant sunflower, calendula, and cosmos seeds.

In September, when I return, I call the breeder in Sedgwick.

"Just one left in the litter. A runt, three months old. He's red and white. Come and take a look."

I phone Clint and Varney in Massachusetts. "I'm going to look at a corgi puppy," I report.

"Well, you know you can't just 'look' at a puppy," Clint says. "It'll be love at first sight. Bring some dog biscuits and a blanket."

I catch a glimpse of a great big windjammer tacking under the bridge as I drive over it in my mother's old Chevy Malibu. On the front seat beside me are a clean, white, threadbare flannel sheet, my grandmother's initials sewn in one corner, and a box of Milk-Bone dog biscuits.

As I turn onto the dirt road leading to the Bagaduce River and the corgi breeder, I fret whether the sheet will be soft enough, the dog biscuits the right brand. I fret whether I've gone daft.

"Dwarf herders, that's what corgis are," says Gary, the breeder, as he welcomes me at his back door. "Built short to avoid the kick of a cow. And they're smart—good companions."

The puppy lies in a commodious, comfortable crate, door open, at one end of Gary's kitchen. With his rubescent coat and deep white chest, left front paw sweetly folded under right, he's a masterpiece out of Velázquez or, closer to home, Sargent.

"What's his name?" I ask, unable to take my eyes of that foxy, impish, little face.

"He doesn't have a name yet," Gary says.

"At three months old?" I ask. I note how his translucent, pointed ears, lightly edged in black, play about, sensitive to our talk.

"The new owner should name him," Gary says.

"Is he housetrained?"

"Partly."

"I don't know. . . . That might be a problem," I say.

I edge sideways to a window. At the end of a feathery field, the Bagaduce River surges on its passage to Penobscot Bay. I think of my busy life in New York. I'd have to take him out before breakfast and at lunchtime, down thundering streets, and late at night, after the opera, among dope dealers and robbers.

"How would he do in New York, d'you think?" I say.

"Oh, he'd do fine. Corgis are feisty, adaptable. No problem."

I sit down on a red chair by the crate.

"Can I hold him?" I ask.

Gary places him in my lap. The puppy licks my thumb, sucks on it. His wet nose snuffles between my fingers. Dark, bewitching eyes, as if rimmed with eyeliner, fix on me. Little red tufts mark his eyebrows.

On the ride home, he curls up on the white sheet, his long, slightly arched nose resting on his white paws.

"Would you like a drink of water?" I say. Gary had given me a plastic soda bottle filled with water and a Styrofoam bowl.

As we cross over the bridge, he closes his eyes and whimpers.

"Maybe a biscuit?"

Traversing the S-shaped causeway between Little Deer Isle and Deer Isle, I turn to the small, round, furry ball next to me on the passenger seat and place my hand tentatively on his tiny tummy. "You must have a name, dear little thing," I say. I remember a conversation I overheard the other day between two women in a pizza restaurant in Blue Hill. They sat at a small table next to mine.

"Jumeau," said the one in a long cotton skirt and sandals.

"Juno?" said the other one, in a purple peasant blouse.

"No, Jumeau, as in Alaska."

"Isn't it *Juneau?*"

"Is it?" They bit into their slices, made with salmon.

"I prefer Juno, as in the goddess."

Silence.

"It's for a girl, right?"

"Junoesque, she ain't." The woman in the long skirt lifted a piece to her lips.

"But in a couple of years . . ."

"Anchovy maybe. Chovy for short." She waved her cheesy slice. "Or Jack. My dad was called Jack. Mac and I talked names in the car from Boston. Five hours. Wouldn't let him open his mouth unless he had a name in it. He wanted to discuss the election of

Corazon Aquino. Then our kids."

"Jack for a *girl*?"

"Yeah, Mac didn't love it, either."

"You bought a house on Deer Isle?"

"Mmm—we're here to close on it."

"You didn't talk about *that*? Or Mikhail Gorbachev? Jacques Chirac?"

"Jacques!"

"Jacqueline!"

"You could go with Lady, or Muffin."

"Jumeau!"

"Jumelle!"

I look at the red puff beside me. "You know what? We gotta get thinking . . ."

We follow the road south to the village of Deer Isle. From there we drive two and a half miles along the twisting, country road to my house. The wind howls around the corners of it as we approach, shaking the shutters. The little dog's golden red and white body quivers beside me.

"We're home, *mon ami*," I say.

He places his paws on the passenger door's armrest and peers out the window.

What does he see? I wonder.

I carry the warm, sweet parcel of fur onto the porch and remember how Ronnie always scurried about among my family's leather- and canvas-shod feet.

"You'll be scampering yourself soon," I say.

With the tiny creature curled up in my arms, his face hidden on my chest, I think back to the times I came onto this porch as a very young child, held by Georgette, my Swiss nurse, my face hidden against her chest in much the same way. And the times I held my doll Rosie nestled tight against me.

"Dites bonjour à tes tantes et tes oncles et ta grandmère," Georgette had said in her high, operatic, Bidu Sayao voice.

I place him on the porch floorboards, next to one of the old steamer chairs, which I recently painted to match the fresh coat of spruce green on the house trim. "Come, little one." I beckon him to the French doors into the living room. But he goes kerplunk onto the boards, doesn't budge.

I must name him, I think.

"Come," I repeat. "This is your *home*."

I fall to my knees. "Good little boy," I say. I kiss him between the eyes.

He wriggles, then lowers his chocolate eyes charmingly. I pick him up once more and sweep him into the house.

"There's the fireplace, the dining table, the books, the ship models." I swirl him around the living room so he can see everything.

He nuzzles my neck. A few red hairs float up and settle on my cheek.

Attababy!

"There's the view—the Camdens, Butter, and Bradbury." I pirouette in front of the windows with their old, wavy panes facing west.

He gazes into my face.

Was I like this with Georgette, my Swiss nurse? Small, frightened, silent?

I walk into the kitchen, past the piles of Canton and Worcester dishes in the pantry, and lower him gently to the floor.

"Want something to eat?" Gary had given me a small bag of dried puppy food. I place a few tablespoons in a bowl on the floor next to the sink. He doesn't move for a minute, then inches toward the bowl and tentatively crunches on the nibbles.

"Hurrah!" I say.

He waggles his tail-less rump and takes a few additional morsels.

"Attababy!"

He licks his lips and tries on a corgi smile.

"Let's go meet the ghosts."

I coax him back into the living room. He pads softly, shyly across Eleanor's rose and umber hooked rug, and bumps against a wicker chair in which Eleanor's apparition, in a sunflower yellow and turquoise print shirtwaist dress, turns the pages of one of her ever-present FDR histories.

"Heavens, Brenda, what have we here?" she says, reaching down to massage the puppy's ears.

My uncle John is seated in his usual place, the Morris chair to the right of the fireplace. His mustache quivers on his upper lip as he makes his way through *Yachting Wrinkles: A Practical and Historical Handbook of Valuable Information for the Racing and Cruising Yachtsman*, by Captain A. J. Kenealy, published in 1890.

Wakened from his fireside slumber, Ronnie is startled, unsure how to behave. He stands up, his tail rigid.

On the sofa, Grandma and Dorothy contemplate the cold, dark fireplace.

"'Dark as a wolf's mouth,'" Grandma says to Dorothy, quoting Sir Walter Scott.

"You need a name, little fella," I say to the new puppy.

Tentatively, he steps in Ronnie's direction.

"Wasn't your nickname in school 'Bracey?'" I say to Eleanor.

The pup rolls on his back right in front of Ronnie.

"Bracey!" I say.

He jumps up, faces me attentively, a more assured tilt to his nose.

"Well, I never had a *dog* named after me . . ." Eleanor grumbles uncertainly.

"I've brought Bracey home to meet the family," I say reprovingly. "Please help him feel comfortable."

Dorothy moves her fingers lightly over the sofa's upholstery, as if playing Mozart on a spinet. Bracey trots over to nibble them.

"I miss my Pekingese, Ming-Toe-Swivel-Hips," John says suddenly. He reaches over to rub the black mask of Bracey's forehead.

"I could light a fire!" I say.

Eleanor blanches.

"Oh, Bracey," I say. "What if it smokes?"

Bracey watches me between finger nibbles.

"*I'll* do it," Eleanor says.

Bracey moves closer to the hearth, blocking her way. He lies down, his nose tucked between his paws.

"No, I'll do it!" I say.

I place crumpled-up pages from the *New York Times* in the fireplace, add kindling and a spruce log.

Bracey curls up tight on the hearthrug. John peers fondly at him over the top of his glasses. Once, in my late teens, on one of our sails, I'd asked him, "What was I like when I came here as a baby?" "I don't remember," he'd said. "I never noticed you. Never knew you were here. You were *toujours* with Georgette."

The fire catches slowly—first the paper, next the kindling, finally the log, flare.

Their faces illuminated in the glow, John twinkles, Dorothy gazes incuriously into the red embers, and Grandma smiles delicately.

"Good job," Eleanor says, though she can't help rising to tweak ever so slightly one stray twig in the construction.

"We did it!" I say to Bracey.

He wags his rump.

"We have to go back to New York for the winter, you know," I tell him. "I have work there, and a lover. But you'll like it, I hope. We'll stroll in Central Park. Maybe you'll make a few friends."

Bracey and me beside the fireplace

Through a window, I see a gull drop a mussel down onto the rocks.

"And we'll run around the reservoir."

The family drifts up the stairs.

I put on another log. I sit down beside Bracey on the rug in front of the fire; he uncurls his body and I stroke his tummy.

⇁ 4 ↼

MUSETTA'S WALTZ

After closing up the house for the winter, I bring Bracey back to New York with me in my Chevy Malibu. On his first afternoon as an Upper West Sider, he takes a walk with me in our neighborhood, along Ninety-third Street between Amsterdam and Columbus avenues. Brownstones and pre-war apartment buildings line the street across from the looming Joan of Arc High School, palely lit by the angling sun. All is quiet, even the school, where students must be in the middle of classes. He sniffs the plane trees and maples that manage to rise out of their dirt patches along the sidewalk.

When we reach Columbus Avenue, horns blare, sirens shriek, and the No. 7 bus lumbers to a thundering stop at the corner. Bracey halts in his tracks and begins to tremble. He peers up at me, eyes dark with panic. I crouch on my knees and put my arms around his chest. Caressing his ears, I whisper into them, "It's okay, honeybun." Quivering and cringing, he tries to turn back. "It's noisy, but completely safe, sweetie pie," I say. A woman with a shopping bag and a fat beagle pauses by our side.

"Is your doggie all right?" she asks.

"He's a country puppy," I say. "He'll be fine. Thanks."

"Oh, yes, poor little thing. Jasper didn't like the city at first, either. Good luck."

Bracey's shaking lessens after a moment or two. He composes himself and breathes air into his chest. Raising his head, he begins to observe his surroundings. I lead him south on Columbus Avenue, past a drycleaners with an elderly tailor sewing at the front of the store. A dress shop next door has a display of pastel-colored knit scarves and shawls draped over baggy jeans. An optician flaunts designer sunglasses. Along the way, people smile at Bracey, and bend to pat him. "What is he?" they ask. (Interestingly enough, on the East Side, everyone knows immediately what he is.) He begins to relax. A woman and her schnauzer enter a pet store nearby, where Lab puppies lie sleeping in the window. Bracey slows to gaze at them, alert. Pressing on, he finds the pluck to greet a lively, brown poodle, who sniffs him intimately. A few feet beyond, he suddenly stops and sits to stare at a pretty, nut-brown dachshund tied up in front of a deli, waiting for her owner. He's spellbound. "Oh, Bracey, she's lovely!" I say.

The high point of Bracey's day becomes our morning walk around the Central Park Reservoir. Counting the crosstown blocks to the park and the approach over paths and hillocks to the reservoir, it's a good two miles, round trip. On a chilly November day, I see an Afghan on the brow of a hill to the north of the reservoir. The west wind ruffles his silky hair, teases his delicate, long topknot. Outlined against the early morning sky like Heathcliff on Dartmoor, he stares intently into the distance.

I'm always on the lookout for a friend for Bracey or a playgroup that won't treat him like an outsider. "Here's a pal for you," I tell Bracey. "He's big, but he appears to be a bit thoughtful; a bit sensitive, maybe."

We climb the hill. Still focused elsewhere, the Afghan ignores us. But directly over the rise, in a delicious, small hollow surrounded by great oaks and maples, a dozen dogs—bearded collies, shelties, Jack Russells, mutts—are in an ecstasy of roughhousing, hurling themselves at one another and running for balls or Frisbees, mad with the joy of sociability. I can't believe our luck!

At one end of the hollow, people stand facing the dogs. I'm not used to befriending strangers. I feel shy. For Bracey's sake, though, I make the effort. Leaving the Afghan behind, we descend into the vale, Bracey, at first, like me, hanging back slightly. He can see this isn't an opportunity for herding, his true calling. The playing field is a muddy pit, a cauldron of furry legs and paws, snapping jaws. Leaves are everywhere, tossed into the air like snowflakes in a February blizzard. Bracey looks up at me, less than certain.

"Go on. Go in there," I urge. He heads into the maelstrom, crouching as low as he can, nose to the ground.

Meanwhile, I wonder what on earth these seasoned, sophisticated New Yorkers in their Adidas, wide-shouldered parkas, and becoming fedoras talk about as they watch their dogs.

I edge up closer. No one turns around.

"She won't eat her Iams mini-chunks. Scatters them on the kitchen floor," a young man with shaved head and woolen aqua scarf says.

"Sascha didn't eat his mini-chunks for five days. Give her time," says a woman in a lilac jacket.

"Last night, Sheba shredded the *Book Review* section of the *New York Times*," says a heavyset man in a business suit. "My mother was over for dinner. She was hysterical. 'Is this the way you're bringing her up?' she asked me."

And then I hear, "Look, there's a corgi! Such a beautiful corgi! A puppy! Where'd he come from?" Spinning and pirouetting, Bracey is suddenly smack in the center of the galvanic storm of barks, woofs, snarls.

"Oh, he's mine!" I offer, ready to be witty, informative, anything they wish.

"He's gorgeous." "How old is he?" "What's his name?" "Where'd you get him?" they ask, still with their backs to me.

I watch the dogs surround Bracey, snuff him, cuff him. Delirious with happiness, his long muzzle opened wide with passionate, jubilant barking, he's Otello crying "Esultate" after his victory over the Turks. King of the moment, he's the newest—and the handsomest, I can't help thinking—guy on the block.

"Five months," I say. "His name's Bracey."

"He's a baby—what a love! How much does he weigh?"

From then on, I look forward to our daily circuit of the reservoir, among the swarms of joggers and walkers. Quite a few people say hello to Bracey by name. "How ya feelin', Bracey, hon?" a thin, blonde jogger in a cherry-striped hat halloos as she goes by. He

Woodcut I did depicting Bracey in New York.

swaggers a bit, his fetching, little bottom waggling in three-quarter time. Makes me proud. We're part of a community, I realize.

Speaking of three-quarter time, one afternoon, while I'm editing the catalog of the Peggy Guggenheim Collection, I hear "Musetta's Waltz" from *La Bohème* on the radio. I'd been reminiscing out loud recently to Bracey about how I'd waltzed as a girl in long, white tulle dresses at balls in the Plaza Hotel in New York.

"I was a debutante," I told him. "Sometimes I took four boys in tuxedos with me to a dinner party and on to a dance. Years later, I even waltzed in Kashmir—in the old British colonial clubs with UN peacekeepers." And suddenly it occurs to me: "Why, Bracey, I'll teach you to waltz!" Bracey's in his bed under my desk. "Will you dance with me?" I ask, poking my head under the desk. He doesn't move. In circuses, wearing clown hats and tutus, corgis jump through hoops and do tumbling acts, but waltz? "D'you hear me?" I say. "May I have this dance?"

At last, I drag him out and hold him upright by his forepaws.

His back legs give out. I pick him up—he's gained weight in the months we've been in New York, must be close to thirty pounds—and whirl him around the living room, bedroom, and kitchen until I'm dizzy. He seems to like the rhythm, the one-two-three beat. He certainly appreciates being held tight.

All winter, we dance to waltzes on the radio—to the "Blue Danube Waltz" and the waltzes in the *Nutcracker*. One evening, as I'm cooking spaetzle noodles on the stove in the kitchen, I hear the waltzes from *Der Rosenkavalier*. I can never resist them. I pick Bracey up from the cracked linoleum floor and float with him around the living room, past the antique lowboy and French marble-top. When Kurt Moll, as the drunken Baron Ochs, sings the waltz at the end of Act II, I collapse on the sofa and sob about how gorgeous and perfect the music is. Bracey lies in my arms, his head against mine, patiently waiting for my operatic flood to subside.

Over the next few years, I fret about which is our home—New York or Deer Isle. Bracey and I continue to spend our winters in New York—and increasing portions of our summers on Deer Isle. While I find myself troubled more and more about which place I'd rather be in, Bracey adapts equally to life on Deer Isle and in the city. In my small apartment, he stakes out his territory in the tiny hall with the oak washstand, where he lies with his ears twitching at the noises of tenants talking and slamming doors in the building. Or he reposes in a corner of the outmoded kitchen, which smells of onion and detergent, where he watches me make chick-pea *pullao* and listens to dogs bark on the street below. Or he lounges under my desk in the bedroom, where he hears my pencil scratch over piles of heavy-duty, art-historical papers written by scholars.

He makes friends with Lewis, the day doorman, who grins, scratches his ruff every time we enter or leave the building, and asks, "How's tricks, Bracey, old boy?" Impresario of alternate side-of-the-street parking on our block, Lewis, in his uniform with epaulettes, masterminds the shifting of cars as elegantly as Seiji Ozawa conducts the Boston Symphony. Included in this production is the old family Chevy Malibu (which I bring to the city to help in transporting Bracey). The Chevy has a creamy, rounded roof and assertive body—a rolling chassis with marmoreal contours—and a ton of chrome.

I leave Bracey alone in the apartment when I go to the Metropolitan Opera with my lover, who is a widower and visits from out of town. Before the performances at the Met, we often eat in the area. He holds my arm as we stand poised on the sidewalk to cross the maze of avenues to Lincoln Center. It's important to choose the right spot and moment to navigate to the opera house—lit up like a liner at night breasting an angry, metallic sea—or we'll be struck down by waves of hooting automobiles.

One night, he and I climb the three flights to the Dress Circle to see *Elektra*. Just before the house lights dim, I see the crystal chandeliers rise and disappear above the overhang of the Dress Circle, like nets of sparkling herring hoisted up the side of a trawler.

The curtain swings open on a scene of women servants in the palace of Agamemnon, Elektra's father, who was murdered by her mother, Klytemnestra. Hildegard Behrens, as Elektra, runs on stage, long red hair streaming behind her, a ranting, unhinged gypsy. Kill, *kill*, she sings, dancing in menacing, insane circles on the big paving blocks.

I shift my focus from her figure to the orchestra in the pit, close my eyes, feel myself lifted into wild, lashing treetops. The strings slither away from the swirling universe of voices—Chrysothemis, Klytemnestra, Orest—violins and violas dive down where the brasses feed, where the voices begin, dropping chords into swirling pools, pine needles into a rushing creek: no sun, half-light darkening to strangled black. Oboes, trombones, and flutes shine in the stream. Their notes skim rocks, slip over stones, melt on sand, parting and colliding with the voices seeking entry into the roots of tall trees. The voices resonate through hollow trunks, burst into the maelstrom of skittering instruments high up, and blend with reeds vibrating in the wind. I feel wild myself and imagine swimming up through the dark tunnels to salt-splashed sunlight.

The feathering strings separate again from the voices, plummet, renew the cycle—my cycle of revelation, a new sensibility. I experience this new intensity, this ecstasy, and safely return. Moving my shoulder against my lover's in the seat beside me, I touch him for reassurance.

I lean over the railing to see the orchestra properly, to hear the clarinets and horns stop the flow of strings, the strings escape the voices and take their suicidal leap.

In her final, stamping waltz, Behrens's microscopic figure is a torch of Hellenic hatred and ghastly emotion. Not Bracey's and my comforting waltz. Klytemnestra will be killed, Elektra will die.

Drugged by the lurid world, drunk on brutal chords, I almost pass out. The house is silent, mesmerized by her performance, her murderous intentions.

On the tiny stage, Behrens gestures and dances furiously to the recurring strains of the waltz. I can't watch the killing scene, even if it's out of sight in the palace. I hunch down in my seat, at the edge of a precipice. I sink lower for protection, anything to avoid the scene below. Why is this affecting me so deeply? Let Orest kill Klytemnestra. I shall hear the agonized cries, the brilliant clashing of cymbals and the brutal din of kettledrums. The slaughter is not mine. Elektra shall collapse and die as she dances.

It's for precisely this kind of experience—shattering though it may be in the case of *Elektra*—that I attend the opera. I attend for the all-encompassing exaltation and exhilaration offered by this art. My lover, with his bright, kindly face, puts his hand over mine, and together we listen. Can I give him up? As I would have to do, were I to relocate permanently to Maine. Can I give opera up?

Late that night, I return to my apartment to find Bracey waiting in the hall, as usual. I take him out to Amsterdam Avenue, where the drug dealers and hangers-on now congregate on the west side of the avenue, pushed there by an armed guard hired to patrol the avenue's east side. The dealers and I acknowledge each other with polite expressions. Bracey trots by them, saucy and brave.

$\rightleftharpoons 5 \rightleftharpoons$

PATTERNS IN ICE

It's early spring, and Bracey and I are making one of our twice-yearly trips to Maine in the Chevy. Chewing on a spongy toy moose, Bracey lounges next to me in the ample passenger seat. "My doll Rosie and I sat in a steamer chair," I say to him, "on a big ocean liner, the *Georgic*, going to England in 1937, when I was eight, a mere pup like you, dear heart." My hand off the wheel for a second, I feather his forehead with my fingers. Bracey and I make these trips between New York and Deer Isle much the way I did as a child between England and the U.S. In fact, we're on our way to get the house ready for renters. With all these voyages, the seasons begin to mark the years for me, the years to slip into one another.

"How come you seem to adjust to these voyages better than I do?" I say to Bracey, as he works away at the moose's floppy antlers. "You appear to take all this back-and-forthing in happy stride." Or

Cunard-White Star liner RMS Georgic

does he? He stops chewing suddenly and stares at me with his dark brown eyes. Maybe he's just as confused as I used to be as a child—and, frankly, continue to be. Am I doing to Bracey what my parents did to me, endlessly dragging him to and fro? He keeps his eyes on me, a reflective expression on his face.

"Funny," I say, "I always needed Rosie when I traveled. I loved her the best of all my dolls." Maybe it was her hairiness, I think, as I reach over—keeping my eye on the road—to rough up Bracey's white chest; her animality, her oddity. Rosie's whole body, including her squarish arms and legs, was covered with fuzz. I used to bury my face in her aromatic, pink fur. Quickly glancing at him out of the corner of my eye, I poke him gently in the stomach. "She was all fur," I say, "like you." Right now his fur smells of New York—of pavements and fuel—but soon enough it will be salty and fresh.

At Portsmouth, we drive on the bridge (Bracey and I singing together—*a tutti passage!*) high over the Piscataqua River—into Maine. I stop in Kittery for lunch, and let Bracey out for a pee and short walk in the welcoming, brisk air. Back in the car, I offer Bracey a biscuit. He grabs it out of my hand, without so much as a thank-you. I refill his traveling bowl with fresh water at the Kittery Trading Post water fountain.

On the road again, I go on in greater detail to Bracey about my 1937 crossing to England. "My mother wore a cloche hat, angled over her brow, and my father, a tie and vest," I say to Bracey. "They sat in steamers next to mine. My mother sewed a dress for Rosie." The whole scene comes back to me as I drive along the highway. My mother had a remote elegance about her—a vigilant stillness. Nevertheless, I summoned the courage to say, "Mummie, you make the sleeves and skirt so short! Rosie's arms and legs look even fluffier that way."

"Darling, I thought that's what you loved about Rosie—her furriness. But it certainly makes it hard for me to fashion proper dresses. Just think, if I were making a dress for Shirley Temple."

Shirley, with her blond corkscrew curls, was home in England with my other dolls.

"Shirley doesn't need another dress," I said.

"But she's so pretty! I'd like to make her a yellow dress with a deep blue collar," my mother said, longingly.

I mull over the conversation with my mother as Bracey and I travel north on 95, through forests of pine and spruce. My mother and I had problems over Rosie, I see that clearly now. She'd even left Rosie behind in England two years earlier, when we'd come to the U.S. the summer I was six. I didn't discover it until we were aboard ship. We were always leaving things behind, no matter in which direction we went: relatives or dogs in America; governesses and nannies and dolls in England. On this occasion, I cried so long my mother cabled my governess, Miss Middleton, who was staying with her family in Sussex, ship-to-shore. Miss Middleton dutifully telephoned her nephew in Norfolk, who took the train to Roehampton. He wrapped Rosie in tissue paper and newspapers, put her in a cardboard box, and mailed her to me on Deer Isle.

On the ship's deck, a steward in white uniform with gold on the shoulders and black shiny shoes served the two of us hot bouillon, I recall. I propped Rosie's soft body against my chest and held the gold-rimmed china cup in both hands.

"Rosie, would you like a sip of broth?" I whispered politely, raising the cup to her little red lips. Her face, the only non-woolly region on her person, was painted canvas: cornflower blue eyes, rosebud mouth, round red spots on her cheeks. Yellow strands fell from under her bonnet to one side of her forehead. Over the top of her head, I saw the sea spreading out forever: dark cinnamon close in, glimmering sapphire on the horizon. And high above us, the ship's two huge funnels soared into the scudding skies.

While my mother sewed, my father read the ship's newspaper aloud. There would be a children's Ping-Pong tournament at 1 p.m., a tea dance at 4 p.m., horse racing (with cutouts of horses on stands) at 9 p.m.

Dad aboard ship

"May I play in the Ping-Pong tournament?" I asked.

As we roll by fields shafted by sunlight, I tell Bracey I'd become good at Ping-Pong after all our crossings. He's half asleep. On board ship, my skill contributed a frisson of savoir faire, a boost to my always irregular confidence. (Many years later, I recollect, when I was eighteen and returning with friends from a summer in Europe on the *Mauritania*, I won a tournament partnered—by lot—with the famous violinist Nathan Milstein. In the bow, as the ship entered New York Harbor, he gave me a strong handshake and said, "You're a grand slammer.") "Rosie liked to watch me play Ping-Pong," I say to Bracey. "Bet you would, too!"

"We'll have lunch shortly," my mother answered as she stitched. "We'll try to be finished in time for the tournament."

"Oh, I do so want to play!" I said.

The day before, I'd played Ping-Pong with two Argentine girls and a Swiss boy. I'd carried Rosie with me and sat her on a pile of paddles. "Such a funny doll!" one of the girls said. "Why do you sit it there?"

"So she can watch me play," I said.

"¡Si, claro!" she laughed as she hit a fabulous shot right to the edge of the table.

The children, veteran transatlanticers like me, were equally skilled at the sport. We hit the ball back and forth with furious enthusiasm. "Pip pip!" I shouted. They didn't seem to notice my English accent or the English pleated woolen skirt I wore in late August.

After the Ping-Pong game, which I'd won by a hair's breadth, I held Rosie tight as we hung over the railing and gazed at sharks in the sea a hundred feet below, much as we did the more amiable porpoises in Penobscot Bay.

In her steamer chair, my mother calmly went on sewing while she waited for the ship's luncheon gong to be struck. The wind off the water blew the light cotton fabric of Rosie's new dress-in-the-making, with its pattern of tiny green swimming ducks, into furls around my mother's long fingers. I think of that moment all those years ago as I drive my mother's car under the high cumulus clouds stretching out westward.

I remember another scene of her sewing—this time in our apartment living room in Roehampton Close, near London, shortly before our journey back to the States that same year. We lived on the upper floor of a cluster of two-story buildings set in spacious gardens. "Darling," she'd said. "I'm shortening your navy blue pleated skirt, so you can wear it in the States." The tops of chestnut trees through the windows framed her thick, wavy brown hair and her finely carved mouth. She sat on a plum-purple chaise longue. I was in love with her beauty. Helplessly suspended before it, I was fearful, too—of the ferocity hidden beneath her benevolence.

She reached inside a small, reddish, leather-covered sewing chest in the shape of a bombé commode, which stood on a low table beside her, for a thimble, needle, and thread. Tiny compartments held a yellow satin pincushion, spools of thread, buttons, and booklets of needles. In the drawer was an exquisite pair of scissors with a motif of climbing roses on the blades, and a silver measuring tape. The sewing chest was as clean and neat as any medical laboratory. I never became adept at sewing myself, whether out of rebellion against or in awe of her precise, surgeon-like mastery of the delicate instruments. A finely embossed brass plaque in the lid's center showed a scene of a woman sitting under a willow, hand to her chin, communing with a dog. Slender, sad, she reminded me of my mother. I smelled the lavender water on my mother's wrists as she raised the needle to eye level, moistening the blue cotton filament with her lips and threading it with precision. She measured, cut, and stitched with speed and accuracy.

"I don't mind doing this," she said, taking the scissors from the drawer and snipping the thread, though I hadn't even thought to ask her if she did. "I want you to look nice."

Bent over her sewing, her mien was wistful.

I watched, feeling confused, anxiously regarding her. And I recall that outside the window, gusts had set the tree branches lunging behind her. Even back then, I now realize, I didn't want to be a bother.

Although tugged by a genuine desire to aid the powerless, my mother also suffered from a feeling of her own helplessness: of inadequacy and uselessness. She didn't want to be a spectator to life. She frequently said she'd wanted to be a doctor, a forlorn dream for a woman of that generation. The closest she came to fulfilling this dream was during World War II, in New York, when she trained to be a Gray Lady, going on to nurse soldiers and sailors with terrible injuries in Bellevue Hospital. "Those years," she said, "were the happiest of my life." Forever after, she would stop at automobile accidents to see if she could help. Once, she dragged an injured man into a nearby house over the protests of the owners: "Out of our way," she ordered. "This man is badly hurt."

But as she sat there stitching my skirt in Roehampton, she seemed to experience a far greater sacrifice. She could have been reading her beloved Brontë sisters, after all, or Edith Wharton or Henry James. Instead, in her long, beige, belted cardigan over a plaid skirt, she worked for me, labored for me.

When my father came home from work, she showed him the skirt. "Look what I did for Bren, look how much I sewed for her today." On cue, my father said, "You are a wonder. The skirt is a miracle."

Tall, slim, brown-eyed, the two of them looming over me, my mother smiling a little, bending toward my father.

I still have this little sewing chest, which holds a place of honor in my living room in Maine. I open it up only occasionally to use its needles and thread to sew on buttons, and, as I do, somewhat clumsily, I think how much she'd have preferred stitching up after an appendectomy in an operating room to sewing Rosie's clothes, or mine. Iron-willed, disciplined, good with her hands, she'd have been an excellent surgeon. And, I suspect, a more receptive mother.

As Bracey and I move along the highway through fields and over hills with long views of the sea and island-sprinkled bays, my thoughts return to the ship crossings, which, I now understand, gave me a life in between continents. I didn't have to deal with the problems of looking and sounding like an English girl in the States or of being an American in England. Accents and clothes didn't matter. Ordinary existence was suspended. My shyness disappeared. I could slam the Ping-Pong ball back and forth—let it fly in the air, wham it back down. I was in my own hemisphere, no foreign, prevailing customs and attitudes to smother me. I could be a princess on a country-less, oceanic roller coaster, a funfair at sea. In my steamer chair in the middle of the Atlantic, I stroked Rosie's downy arms as the great ship took us over the vast depths—home, to England. Now I rub Bracey's ears as we travel in the Chevy between New York and Maine.

In the late afternoon, we reach the island, after crossing the bridge, and drive past pretty white clapboard houses with large barns and green fields. I catch glimpses of dimpled, dark blue water between spruce and pine. The village of Deer Isle has shrunk over the last forty years to a post office, small grocery, gift shop, and two galleries. In the winter, only the post office is open. After the village, at the top of the hill, we turn right onto a country road that leads to a smaller road and, finally, to my driveway. Wayne, my caretaker and contractor, has already opened the house, and the steamer chairs are in place out on the porch. Bracey patters around the living room on the hooked rugs and sniffs under the dining table. He salutes the ghosts with good cheer and a wag of his rump.

"We're home, Bracey, pet," I say.

Camden Hills across East Penobscot Bay

The Camden Hills rest in violet slumber across the water. I walk past the shelves of books and wicker armchairs to the kitchen, where I deposit Bracey's and my provisions on the countertop. The kitchen has a musty smell, overlaid by the scent of pine.

I go to the fridge and put away the eggs, skim milk, and goat cheese. "D'you want your supper?" I ask Bracey, who sits on the linoleum floor, focused on my every action. At the word *supper*, he straightens up, cocks his head left and right, and lets out a yip. "Okay, okay!" I say, as he brushes against my legs. I pour his Iams kibble into his dish. He gobbles it in about one, frenzied minute. Finished, he finds one of his playthings—a furry black and orange owl—and tosses it in the air. A slant of fading sunlight catches the knobby legs of the kitchen table, where I plunk myself to watch Bracey scoot around with his owl.

"You spend too much time playing with dolls," my mother said to Patsy and me, as we sat, surrounded by them, in my bedroom in Roehampton. It was a chilly day in December, I recall, a few months after we'd returned from the U.S. Patsy Pearson was my best friend; we went to the same school in Putney, next to Roehampton. She was Canadian, had blond hair and an oval face. We played dolls almost every day—including tea parties, with Rosie and others—either at my house or hers, which was close by. We were good mothers and hugged our teddy bears and Raggedy Anns. At Patsy's house, her father, who became prime minister of Canada in 1963, played the piano enchantingly by ear—popular tunes like "Good Night, Irene." Underneath his grand piano, engulfed by dolls in fluffy petticoats, babies in miniature strollers, and woolly sheep tied with black yarn, we hardly heard the pinging and thrumming over our heads.

That winter, when I was eight, my mother took Patsy and me and my brother Loring, along with the two sons of English friends, to Crans, a small ski resort in the Swiss Alps, for Christmas. (Johnnie was in school in the U.S.; my father was in the U.S., as well, on business.) "You should be more active, learn to ski in Switzerland, speak French with other children," my mother said. "No dolls," she added firmly. We traveled by steam-engine train from London, across the English Channel by ferry, and then up into the Swiss mountains by train again. From each of our succession of compartment seats, we gazed at the changing view: English fields with horses grazing and neat brick villages, the tall white Dover cliffs and blue-brown Channel seas; French cathedral spires and vast chateaux; and, finally, Swiss chalets and snow-covered peaks.

At suppertime, while passing through France, stewards in white uniforms served us *soupe de poisson, coq au vin,* and *soufflé au chocolat* in the paneled French dining car. The tables were set with heavy train silver. I missed Rosie.

"Je n'aime pas ce poisson," I said, putting down my spoon. "What kind of fish is it?"

My mother, elegant in a Parisian wool suit, eyed me as I hunched over my bowl.

"C'est un turbot," my mother said. "Eat it."

I put my spoon back in the murky, parsleyed broth and swirled it around. "Oui, Maman," I responded. Patsy smiled at me, her blue eyes sympathetic, while the boys smirked. Dusk gathered over the swiftly passing foothills behind their heads. Cows, shadowed in the long after-glow, watched from meadows.

"The *coq au vin* was better, and the *soufflé* better still," I say to Bracey, who, bored with his doll, has been rooting around in his dish for overlooked kibbles. Finished with his quest, he sits on the kitchen floor and listens to me carefully. "Once we'd finished eating in the dining car, Bracey, we were quickly herded—yes, that's correct, sweetheart; you'd have done a far better job!—back to our compartment." The train officials, my mother told us, wanted to drop the dining car off before we left France. I dreaded our arrival in Switzerland. My mother had made plans for Patsy and me to go to a pension for girls. She and the boys would stay in a hotel together. I found this grossly unfair. Why did she keep sending me away—or leaving me places?

After we went to sleep in our compartments, the train halted on a siding, angled on a mountain in a blizzard. We awoke at 7 a.m. to blowing snow, a mad carnival of winds, no mountains or valleys to be seen, just swirling flakes. The morning hours went by. Our berths were made up with clean sheets by a train steward. The train didn't move. We could have stayed there slanted *toujours*, slowly starving.

I was very hungry. I'd never missed my breakfast before.

"Where is our *petit déjeuner*?" I asked.

"There's no dining car, darling," my mother said. "You know that."

Cuffed by the winds, the train creaked and shuddered, like our boats moored off our Deer Isle shore in a northwest gale.

When the storm passed, a steam-engine locomotive with a huge snowplow came down the mountain to rescue us. It also brought a Swiss dining car, but—*quelle horreur*—with supper only! The locomotive maneuvered the dining car from the main track to the siding, where it was hitched with much clatter to the last car on the train.

"Supper?" we cried at the conductor, who entered our compartment to make the announcement.

"I regret the inconvenience, mais il n'y a rien à faire." He bowed briskly and left.

"Pas possible!" we cried some more. No buttered rolls with loganberry jam? No omelettes?

My mother looked at us angrily: "You must behave!"

As the train moved out of the snow bank from the siding to the cleared track, we raced to the dining car just the same and fell on the *fondue* and lamb *à la cuillère* and guzzled the apple juice like famished, parched wolves.

"We ate as fast as you do, Bracey," I say, laughing. I lean down to pick up his dish to wash it. "We survived!" I put the rest of our groceries away—the cans of soup on a shelf and loaf of whole wheat bread in the breadbox in the pantry.

Our trip ended with a funicular ride straight up the mountainside to Crans, I recall. Patsy and I kneeled by the cabin windows and silently watched the perpendicular rock face slide by as we ascended, pulled by a single cable, while the boys ran from side to side, whooping and whistling down into the nothingness. My mother sat quietly, holding her breath.

Crans, a small village with chalets and cafés, was situated on a high, sun-drenched plateau, and surrounded by brilliant ski slopes and glinting skating rinks. With bells ringing, a horse-drawn sleigh drove us to the hotel where my mother and the boys would stay: a tall pink building, covered in balconies, on a snowy slope. Her light-filled room had a balcony overlooking the wide, mountain-rimmed Rhône Valley and a view of peaks from the Matterhorn all the way round to Mont Blanc.

"You and Patsy will be happy at Soeur Frieda's pension, darling," my mother said, patting my cheek a little apologetically. I draped myself on her bed, eyes closed in anguish. "But why can't we be with you?" I watched her unpack her long, velvet bathrobe and light blue slippers and smelled her Chanel No. 5 perfume.

"I was Heidi, orphaned on a Swiss mountain," I say to Bracey, who locates his pad in the kitchen. He circles and digs in it several times before lying down.

Led by my mother, who conducted us through the hotel's hallways and lounges, smiling graciously at the waiters and concierges, Patsy and I returned to the sleigh for the mile ride down to the pension. Patsy's curls whiffled in the breeze as the sleigh descended. Strauss waltzes whirred on a distant megaphone, skate blades cut the atmosphere, sleighs mushed and jingled along snow-packed roads. It certainly wasn't music to my ears; it was a dirge.

"I didn't have you to waltz with, Bracey," I say. He begins to groom his paws. I sit down in a green kitchen chair beside him.

Soeur Frieda, who had dyed-black hair and sharp teeth, met us at the door of the chalet and showed us around the dark, cavernous interior, its long corridors lined with walnut armoires. Upstairs, the three dormitory rooms each had six to eight small, closely spaced cots. With a closed expression on her face, my mother followed Soeur Frieda upstairs and down the halls.

"You'll stay here, mes chéries," my mother said, smoothing my hair. "Vous devez parler français et apprendre faire du ski."

"Au revoir, Madame," she said to Soeur Frieda, waving as the tinkling horses drove her sleigh back up the mountain.

I hated my mother at that moment. I hated Soeur Frieda. I hated Loring for remaining with my mother. I hated the twenty girls—Italian, German, English, Swedish—in their brightly colored woolen snow suits, who banged their skis and shouted in the hallway. I couldn't bear it; I knew I would die. I yearned to be in the hotel with my mother.

"D'you wish to be with me?" I ask Bracey, in his bed. "For always?" I place my hand on his tummy, which softens and goes easy. "I'm always here for you, munchkin." His stubby legs relax. I draw my fingertips along the edge of the dark mask above his eyes. His eyes drift and slowly close.

She'd left me before, of course; perhaps the worst time was when I was three. We were in the States for a year, living in Bronxville. My father had a *depression nerveuse*, and my mother took him to Bermuda to recover. That time, she left me alone for a month with Georgette, my Swiss nurse.

I was so enraged, I stopped speaking French with Georgette entirely, a suffocating knot of anger plugging my throat. I'll fix her, I must have thought. When my mother came home, she was furious! "I want you to be bilingual!" she cried.

"She never forgave me, Bracey, love."

During the ten days we were at Soeur Frieda's pension, my mother came to see us occasionally, if briefly, without the boys, who were busy skiing. She wore a brown gabardine ski jacket with a rose and purple scarf tied at her neck. On one of her visits, I sobbed, "Why did you send me here? I could be with you at the hotel! I could learn to ski just as easily there!"

"How can you talk to me this way?" she said, turning aside. "You don't love me!"

I didn't want to speak French. I didn't want to learn to ski. Patsy skied, but I chose, instead, to skate with one or two other children on the small rink next to the pension. I skated my heart out. I smashed my grief against the exploding white peaks, aiming it like a red billiard ball across a blue glacier, pocketing it in deep holes hidden from the sunlight. I couldn't stop twirling, pirouetting, jumping, the blazing whiteness of the snowcaps tilting in my eyes, the pale sky slanting across my field of vision. "Why don't you ski?" my mother kept asking on each of her visits. I continued my rounds of anguish, my figure eights with the leg first held forward then back, a balancing act of dreams and hurt supported on a steely thin edge, incising patterns in ice, metallic footprints in a gleaming mirror.

One light blue evening, the anger broke and a rhapsodic moment occurred. With Soeur Frieda in the lead, we sledded—for what seemed forever—down the mountain to the valley: two to a sled, through woods and fields, past chalets with goats and cows steaming in snowy yards, across village streets lined by cafés and bakeries, lights coming on as we descended, a procession of small, wooden sleds propelled by airy hands.

"Prenez garde," Patsy shouted whenever we saw a person or a dog on the road. "Prenez garde!" we yodeled as we flew down alpine meadows. I was happy.

Bracey smiles in his sleep. I get up to heat a can of cream of mushroom soup and slice a piece of whole wheat bread for my supper. Thin shafts of fading sunlight penetrate the stands of spruce outside the kitchen window. Finished eating, I rinse my bowl in the sink and put on the kettle. I return to the living room with a cup of tea and take my place on the sofa. Out on the bay, the northwest wind whips the waves to a froth. Giant bouquets of spray explode over Dunham's Ledge.

Bracey jumps up beside me. I grab his muzzle playfully, holding his mouth tight with my fingers. He tries to pull his head away, breathing heavily, then goes still, utterly rigid, his eyes black with distress. He looks as though he's suffocating. "Oh, my God, what have I done to you?" I cry, quickly releasing him. "I'm sorry!" I recognize the symptoms: they're similar to the ones I experienced when I had to wear a gas mask in England during the Munich Crisis of 1938, which occurred after we returned from our last trip to the U.S. The memories of the big, heavy mask on my face—and of feeling smothered and panicky—suddenly overwhelm me. I recall standing in my brown school uniform in the hall of our apartment in Roehampton.

"Darling, you must wear your gas mask to school," my mother said, holding the big, ugly contraption in her hands. "Here, I'll put it on for you."

"But I can't breathe!"

"You must wear it," she repeated, pulling it down over my nose and mouth. On the bus ride with other kids—all of us wearing masks—to my school in Putney, a neighboring suburb of London, the mask pressed hard against my cheeks as I stared through the eyeholes at men and women digging trenches and piling sandbags.

I graze Bracey's forehead gently with the backs of my fingers. He lies on his side, looking reproachful. "Forgive me?" I ask. *Maybe*, he seems to indicate, rolling over on his back for a tummy rub. I hear the wind whistle through the shingles.

My mother wrote a vivid, detailed account of that week-long Crisis in a letter to the family shortly afterward, in October. I found a copy of the letter recently in a box at the back of a closet here. I'm forever on my knees, it seems, scrounging around in musty cavities searching for remnants of my family ghosts.

"Wouldn't you like to visit your aunties in America, darling?" I remember my mother saying to me at breakfast the morning after the first of Hitler's series of threatening speeches. She'd made reservations on the *President Roosevelt* for my brother Loring, who was at school and would meet us at the boat, Miss Middleton, and me. I pierced the yolk of my poached egg with a fork and let it run all over the plate. I was somewhat excited by the possibility, in a way. But I was always going somewhere. Back and forth . . .

According to my mother's letter, my father went to Berlin on business the next day, a dangerous thing to do. While he was there, Hitler announced his refusal to meet with Chamberlain: war seemed imminent. My mother spent the rest of that night trying to reach my father by phone to tell him the troubling news. The following morning, gaunt and exhausted, she sat at her walnut lady's desk in the living room. Peirs, the family cocker spaniel, slept on the beige carpet nearby.

"Daddy will be home soon, darling," she said to me. "But I have more calls to make," she added, distractedly. Her hand shook as she picked up the big black phone. "Go to your room, dear. Miss Middleton will read to you." From my bedroom, down the hall, I

My mother in silk chiffon, with a feather fan

could hear my mother say, "Bitte . . . danke schoen" repeatedly in a hopeless voice.

"Is Daddy all right?" I asked Miss M.

Later that evening, my father, who'd been gone twenty-four hours, at last came home. "Daddy, Daddy, you're back!" I cried as I ran to meet him at the front door; Peirs scuttled behind me.

"But, of course, I am," he said, ruffling my hair with his fingers. "I always come home to you." My mother stood in the doorway to the living room smiling, clearly relieved, though still apprehensive, her eyes darting about.

Unbelievable as it may seem, my parents attended the theater throughout the Crisis. Dressed to the nines, straight out of Noël Coward—my mother in draped silk dresses and chiffon scarves, in a haze of lilac cologne; my father in blue-gray striped suits and a Hamburg—they hurried out into the night.

Naturally, I stayed home with Miss M. Before supper one evening, Miss M., smelling of the thick warm bread she liked to bake, hugged me to her stout body. "Mummie and Daddy will be back soon." Miles away, a siren went off, but abruptly stopped.

"Where is Rosie, sweet Rosie?" Miss M. said. "Bring her to the dining room. She will eat with us."

I ran to my room and picked her up: "Come, Rosie, you're invited to supper!" Miss M. set three places at the table. She drew the green chintz curtains to hide the searchlights in the sky. We ate sausages and mashed potatoes on Worcester plates and drank pink lemonade, but the noise of shovels against gravel and the thunking of sandbags in the garden below made it hard to talk.

"Try not to listen, dear," Miss M. said. "Oh—let's have raspberry fool for dessert."

The phone rang in the living room, and Miss M. answered it. She spoke softly. I couldn't hear what she said. The oak trees in the

Me in my bedroom in Roehampton; Rosie, top right

garden were silent. My parents didn't come home until very late that evening. They were with friends . . . so many friends . . . so many nights out.

The next day, Miss M. dragged my suitcase down from the top of my closet and started to put in blouses and skirts and underwear. "Don't you think she should take the green plaid skirt instead of the navy blue?" my mother asked. "I like her pink flowered blouse so much better than the plain yellow." Odd for her to be fussing about my clothes. Most of the time these days she was either on the phone or listening to the radio in the living room. Miss M. also packed bags for Loring and herself. Peirs and I trailed after her.

"Will I see my aunties?"

"Yes, dear."

"Can I take Rosie with me?"

"Yes, of course."

"Can I take Peirs?"

"No, dear."

"Are Mummie and Daddy coming with us?"

"No, dear."

At 2:30 a.m., long after I'd gone to bed, my fears sufficiently calmed by Rosie, news was broadcast of a settlement. And by 3 a.m., my parents decided there was no longer a need to send us away.

Dusk falls over the bay now, and as the sky darkens, the islands turn ink-black. The wind wanes. I get up to switch on lights, then sit back down on the sofa beside Bracey. "Can you ever pardon me, Bracey, precious?" I ask, caressing the tip of his nose. "I'd never hurt you in a million years." Regarding me with his brown eyes, he rests his head in my lap. An expression of sweet wisdom spreads across his face. His ears play to the sounds of the softening bay. I rub my palm along his back—up and down, up and down. His breathing slows. Mine does, too

⇥6⇤

SKUNK HOUR

Later in June, I'm getting ready for the first tenants of the season to arrive. They're due in six days. I stand on a chair in the kitchen of the Deer Isle house, putting the best china onto higher shelves, out of the renters' reach. Bracey sits at the foot of the chair and regards me alertly. I spot a skunk through the kitchen window. Small, still a baby perhaps, it crosses the driveway to the garage in a strange little loping gait, a wide, white stripe covering its back and tail. Ordinarily, I'd be delighted to think a skunk has taken up residence under the garage—a splash of black and white, a Franz Kline brushstroke—but now? Days before the renters are due?

This year, instead of returning to New York for the summer while the big house is rented, I plan to move with Bracey to the Trivet, the cabin closer to the shore. Designed by my uncle Gerald, after he'd spent a year in architecture school, it was built by my uncles and aunts with their own hands in the 1920s.

The bathroom, added shortly after the original construction by Rodney, the only professional carpenter involved, is crooked on the exterior. The floor, however, is straight on the inside, unlike those in the rest of the cabin, which slope. Rodney, who helped launch the family boats offshore, was often in his cups. His boots had holes in them, "to let the water out," he said. A fixture on Dunham's Point, he lived a mile down the road with his wife and twenty-five cats.

Nobody expected the Trivet to stand more than a few years. But it has been used by family ever since. And, in fact, an old friend of Eleanor's, Elizabeth Otis, who was Gerald's literary agent and, as it happened, John Steinbeck's, spent her summer vacations in the Trivet during the 1950s and 1960s. Tiny, elegant, Elizabeth tottered in her high-heeled, black sandals along "Root 7," Uncle John's name for the bumpy path between the big house and the Trivet, carrying the latest novels by her authors under her arm—perhaps a Reynolds Price or a Walker Percy. When Steinbeck told her he planned a voyage across the country with his poodle companion, this exchange with Elizabeth took place, as quoted in his book *Travels with Charley*:

"Of course you'll stop at Deer Isle."

"It's out of my way."

"Nonsense," she said in a tone I know very well. I gathered from her voice and manner that if I didn't go to Deer Isle I had better never show my face in New York again. She then telephoned Miss Eleanor Brace, with whom she always stays, and that was that.

Yes, *that* was indeed *that*. Fans of *Travels with Charley* continue to come see where George, my aunt's "sulking" cat, so vividly and ferociously described by Steinbeck, once lived. Charley and Steinbeck spent the two nights of their visit in their camper in the driveway, but shopped for and dined on lobster with Eleanor at the family table.

Here, at the main house, I move nineteenth-century red and green Hong Kong pattern dinner plates up to the highest shelves, along with an English Piccadilly honey-glazed-ware luncheon set with garlands of raised green flowers, and a gilded teapot with mauve and rust-colored oriental flowers. My grandparents forked shepherd's pie from these golden bamboo trees (the light from kerosene lamps casting shadows across their serene faces), picked up peas from the plates' birds of paradise, scooped cabbage from their red flowers. As I transfer piles of dishes, moving the Corelle ware down to the bottom shelves for the renters, I'm hurried, resentful. Soon enough I will have moved to my servant's quarters, to my new life as charwoman, daily, landlady.

Bracey, bored with my dish-moving, stretches out on the kitchen floor and sleeps through the clatter.

The next afternoon, while I dust the ship models in the big living room, I spot the skunk again. This time it's headed toward the woods, an adventurer setting out into the forest. I notice the fine white line on her forehead. It's broad daylight, hardly a skunk's favorite hour. Is she ill, rabid? Where on earth is her mother?

I call Dick, a friend who lives a few miles away and has been advising me on gardening matters. "I have a skunk on my property and renters coming in four days," I say.

"Shoot it," he instructs.

"Murderer!" I shriek and hang up.

Bracey seems to want to spend time outdoors at night. He lies by the front door, along its base like the calico Doggie Draft Guards I see in catalogues and think of buying each year. I let him out, wondering at his new inclination, and return to my chores.

I fuss and fume while I scour the downstairs bathroom sink and toilet. Is this crazy, I ask myself, to scrub and wash and tidy a house I can't afford to live in? To move to a doll's house, where everything is miniature, and the floors slope?

Bracey barks at the front door to be let back in. Musing in the hall, not a hair out of place, he keeps his eye on the garage up the driveway, which he can see through the glass door.

The following day, I hear him bark outdoors—gently, quietly for him, not his usual ear-splitting, peremptory baying. Curious about this different expression, I pause from my current project of writing out signs that say *Do Not Use These Cabinets* and walk toward his voice near the seaside garden. And there they are—Bracey and the skunk—standing between a lemon yellow potentilla bush and purple cranes-bill. They're nuzzling.

I hold my breath. They appear to be friends, more than friends. I call out to Bracey in a low voice. He looks at me calmly, but finally, reluctantly, comes to me. I pull him into the kitchen by his collar.

Lover boy Bracey

"Bracey, do you have the remotest idea what you're getting involved in? Have you thought this relationship through?"

Placid, content, he sits dreamily on the clean, shining kitchen floor. Thoughts of exile or dislodgment don't consume him. Nor does the displacement of heirloom platters and teapots distress him. He has discovered a new, refreshing perspective on the world.

I phone the vet.

"I have a skunk on my property and renters coming in three days. What shall I do?"

"Call Richard Eaton," he suggests. "He has a Have-a-Hart trap."

Richard says he'll come at dusk the next day (three days to go!). He'll catch the skunk and take her to a nice wooded area somewhere distant on the mainland and let her go. She'll be fine.

Thank God, I think. Dealing with this latest development is the last thing I have time for. I must get the grass mowed, curtains hung, lamps repaired, beds made . . .

Bracey barks softly by the woodpile. I rush across the rough grass, through the tall spikes of lupine. Large, protective, Bracey looms over the small creature with her chic white stripe. I whisper to him, beckon to him. He walks slowly toward me. Why can't you leave me alone? he seems to say.

My heart aches for him. I'm the mother of a teenager in love with a female from the wrong family—unreliable, dangerously temperamental, perhaps.

But I have a business to run, a house to sustain, ghosts to defy. I work myself into a lather of resentment. The renters will smash the

Skunk Hour

Bracey at his post inside the glass door

china, demolish the ship models, unravel the braided rugs. Without doubt, they will leave the house a smoking ruin: paintings on fire on the walls, bonfires of furniture on the floor, the mahogany doors, charred and glowing, an orange red curtain, blotting out my new life.

The following day, Richard spends two careful, quiet hours locating the skunk, and I follow his progress, moving from window to window, dusting lamps and tabletops, as he prowls the land. In the end, he sights two skunks, male and female, and catches the female.

"Where will you take her?" I ask. "Will she be all right?" She's Bracey's lover, after all.

"I told you. To a nice place."

The day after (one day to go!), he catches the male.

"I'll let him off at the same place I left her, in the woods across the Reach. They're young, brother and sister, probably lost their mother. Ought to be together."

This man cares.

Bracey's hurt, I can see, keeps visiting his trysting places by the seaside garden and the woodpile. That night, he plops himself at the front door and won't budge.

"Try to forget her," I say to him, turning back to the tasks at hand.

I carry my work papers and reference books; my computer and printer; files of unpaid bills and Met Opera folder; tins of muchi curry powder and cumin, bottles of Thai peanut satay, Szechuan spicy stir fry, and garlic tamari sauce; summer cotton t-shirts, flowered rayon skirt, and linen Flax pants and tops; Bracey's Bean bed, dog food, and rawhide chewies—in the garden cart to the Trivet.

I make several trips with the cart through the vegetable and flower beds. Rows of floppily abundant Black Seeded Simpson and Red Sails lettuce intermix with pink and lavender cosmos. How will I water the garden, without the tenants seeing me? Can I crawl on my stomach under the windows, silent and invisible, hose held in my teeth, a serpent in the grass?

All during the move, Bracey remains at his command post on the small deck at the front door of the house. Recovered from his

The Trivet

View of the big house facing the bay

own disappointment, he seems not to share, as I've already noticed, my peevishness at being dispossessed, uprooted. I suppose he'll take up this position even after the renters come, if he feels guests at the big house need to be greeted.

At first, at least, after the renters arrive and Bracey and I set up residence in the Trivet, I have to admit, the cabin is delightful—life is somehow simplified by the small space. I listen to the waves move on the beach at night and to the eiders chattering in the morning. At breakfast, I bring my mug of coffee onto the tiny screen porch and look across the bay to the Camden Hills, observing the mist opening and shutting the view, Hard Head and Butter islands etherealizing into blue, streaming vapors, shifting from substance to dreams. How lucky I am, I decide, to be out here on this quiet, secluded, little point of land.

Then I hear voices on the screened porch at the north end of the big house toward the Trivet, cups and plates rattling on the green-painted table, the Corelle ware, I hope, not the Quimper or Worcester. Clearly, I won't even be able to console myself for my

Seaside garden where Bracey and his sweetheart rendez-voused

reduced circumstances by imagining I'm a rusticator on some un-discovered Down East shore.

All day I hear the tenants—convivial, sociable, wealthy!—talk. I wouldn't be able to avoid eavesdropping if I wanted to, as they regale one another about recent weekends in Budapest, freighter trips around the Horn, treks in Nepal. I rely on their providence to supply me with income to live, these people sitting up on the big porch, my superiors, bosses—isolationists, I can only assume, antiaffirmative-action Republicans, fascists.

When Bracey and I take our evening stroll around the confined circumference of the Trivet, I see them eating dinner downstairs while all the bedroom lights continue blazing upstairs. The house looks like the *Titanic* before she went down, with Bracey and me floating in our small lifeboat, peering across the black water. Dammit, I want to go over there and tell them, turn the *lights off*! I don't, of course. Bracey would do it, but I can't very well ask him.

One morning, I tap on the glass front door of the big house and wait, hand to forelock, for someone to come. Bracey is preoccupied with the crows under the bird feeder searching for leftover birdseeds.

"What can we do for you?" the wife says brightly, holding the door open. She's dressed in navy blue shorts and a white polo shirt, tucked in. "Come in, come in!"

How good she is, I think. Imagine inviting me into this large, clean house. I shall surely muck it up.

"I just want to get a file from my office. I hate to bother you. I'll rush up the backstairs—won't take a minute, and I'll be out of here in a flash."

Don't notice me, I think. Don't watch as I run across your pine floors and up your back stairs to my office, which was once the maid's room with its own back stairs, shut off from the rest of the house. The family always used the front stairs with the thin, elegant Arts and Crafts banister and balusters, but the back stairs are suitable for me.

"I'll only be a minute, I promise," I call back, midway up to my office.

I won't damage anything, I think of adding. I must be careful, not make a habit of coming over here, might want some of the things these spoiled, rich people have. Look at that big, mahogany sideboard. No, don't take the time, I tell myself. I'll be distracted by things, become exactly like the renters with all their possessions. Grab the file on the Penobscot Bay Turtles Investors Club and leave.

Breaking in, that's what I'm doing—well, not exactly, as the owner is standing right there in the hall, she let me in, and she isn't the owner anyway—to get a folder on learning how to buy stocks: I, the poor relation! Paid gardener!

Though I am, in fact, like them. I own this mansion.

From my office window, I look down and see Bracey by the driveway. The activities of black ants in the grass appear to interest him at this moment. Thoroughly engaged, he nevertheless raises his head from time to time to glance around. He has no problems with self-pity, however, has not altered his personality, has managed to hold onto his selfhood. Only my own is in jeopardy.

I rush down the back stairs and out the door with my file.

"Thanks! Thanks! I've got my file," I say. "I'm so grateful to you. What a lovely house," I almost whisper. Stop this!

By the time I get back to the Trivet, I'm breathless. Bracey meanwhile lingers at the big house, doesn't follow me back immediately. He knows his place is there, as it is here, as it is, really, wherever he is.

On the Trivet screened porch I drink another mug of coffee to knock my addled mind back into some sort of order.

Who is the owner of that big house one hundred feet from here? I ask myself. Is it the woman in the navy blue shorts and tucked-in white polo shirt or is it me, sitting here down by the water? I imagine myself at the dining table whipping the tenants with the placemats, holding the ends with my two hands and flapping them at their faces, leaving marks on their cheeks, yelling, "Turn off the lights upstairs! Do it right now. Up the stairs you go! Pronto!" And the tenants clump up the backstairs, wailing and nervous. I see all this from my little porch in the Trivet.

⇥7⇤

CORGI ANGELS IN THE SNOW

Early winter, the tenants by now gone for ages, and Bracey and I are back in the big house—in the kitchen, the warmest room in the house. I seem to be staying on here. But for how long?

There's a message on my machine from Suzy, a friend in New York: "I have a ticket for you for *Tristan* on December 13. Where are you?"

"Shall we remain until Christmas?" I say to Bracey. "D'you think we can survive without insulation?"

A month ago, I bought a lustrous, wine-red Jøtul woodstove, which puts out a velvety, swaddling whiff of heat in the kitchen. Bracey scratches a circle of his own in his round, Black Watch L. L. Bean dog bed by the woodstove.

I call Suzy: "Maybe you'd better give my ticket away," I say to her machine. I put another log in the woodstove.

The wind rattles the windows, whistles through them, shakes the sashes. Slammed by gales all winter, knocked about like an ocean liner at sea, the house shudders and quivers in tune with elemental forces that can only be called Wagnerian: a steady bass roar of waves in the bay overlaid by staccato gusts hitting the corners of the house.

My bedroom extends out over the north porch into the very teeth of the northwest wind, which blasts head on from across the water toward the house and spumes all around the island, pushing huge white breakers before it. The wind wallops the porch with a relentless, upward thrust of air that passes through the porch ceiling and up into the floorboards of my bedroom.

I hate ever to open the door to the bedroom, the cold and dark-

Shadows on the frozen ground; Eagle and Hard Head in the distance

ness immediately clawing at me. I could easily sail one of our tiny ship models across the drafty floor. One evening, I decide to make more of a winter bed for Bracey and me. "Perhaps a cozy bed will help," I say to him.

He watches me as I fetch blankets and sheets from chests and closets and pile them on the bedroom floor. He lies on the pile, grumbling when I pull a blanket out from under him, but subsequently repositions himself. First, I lay a blanket on the bare mattress, a flannel sheet over it, then a bottom sheet, a top sheet, an electric blanket, another blanket, and, finally, another flannel sheet so Bracey's hairs don't get over everything. The bed is now something of a club sandwich, and at its foot is my new queen-size quilt, which I'll pull up a little at a time depending on the temperature. It'll probably end up over my head before the night is through.

After I've installed myself between all of these layers in my green plaid pajamas and wool socks, Bracey jumps on the bed. He doesn't like the noise of wind in the bedroom at night and often retreats downstairs to his bed in the kitchen, away from the wind's whacks and whistles. But this time he remains all night, sleeping restlessly with his ears back, eyelids and whiskers constantly twitching. It's crowded with Bracey on this bed, but he seems not to notice, extending himself on top of his flannel sheet alongside me the way he must have as a puppy with his mother. In fact, he makes a rather good hot water bottle. Whenever I turn over and draw up my knees, he growls softly as my position shifts, then switches around to put his head on my hip, his rear end hanging over the edge of the bed, adjusting soon enough.

A few days ago, all the pipes in the house froze. It was my turn to host the Morning Deer Isle Writers' Group; I'm trying to see if I can learn to write creatively: nonfiction, essays, memoir, whatever. Back in New York, I wrote a monthly column for *SHOW Magazine*, where I worked for two years. And I did a stint at American Heritage producing histories of various states. During my ten years at Praeger Publishers—in between signing up authors at academic and museum conferences and, eventually, running the whole Art Books Division—I found time to write flap and catalog copy. I also livened up dry, erudite art history texts.

Now I write the first thing that comes into my head. In fact, only the week before at the writers' group meeting, I wrote about a splinter under my nail. How I couldn't fit tweezers far enough under the nail to tweak it. How I slid a piece of paper under to see if it would wiggle the splinter. How I even slipped in a piece of oily lettuce leaf to see if it might provide a greasy exit, but only succeeded in adding another bit of debris. The tip of my finger was becoming like the bottom of the sea, with leftover souvenirs of exploration dotted about in a translucent subterraneanscape. "Hey, come again with that last word?" the group cried in unison.

"How talented you are," I used to dream of people saying to me. "You write like Dorothy Parker; paint like Rosa Bonheur." I wanted to hear stuff like that. I still do. Even though I'd never be able to believe a word of it.

Do I want to stay in this blustery house year round?

"It's thirty-five degrees in my kitchen!" I screamed at 6 a.m. to one of the writers on the phone. It took me three hours to defrost the pipes with a hair drier before the writers arrived at 9 a.m. The only heat was coming from the woodstove. If I so much as opened a cabinet door, I was hit by an icy draft.

The other afternoon, I plugged up some cracks in the kitchen walls with fiberglass insulation. Bracey began to chew the spumy pink puffs. "No! Not for doggies," I said. "They're poisonous!" I tugged them from his mouth and put them on a countertop.

I hung pale green quilted bedspreads in the doorways, draped red-plaid Hudson Bay blankets on the chairs, and spread hooked and braided rugs on the floor. Soon the kitchen looked like an antique New England version of a Turkish tent.

"And what are you doing?" I said to Bracey as he stood, motionless, at his water bowl. Eventually, I noticed the water was frozen.

"Oh, poor baby," and set to boiling water to pour over the ice.

In no time it cooled enough for him to drink.

"I'm living an experiment," I told the writers when they arrived.

Did I want to stay in this house year round, meeting its challenges?

"Is it *crazy* to inhabit this big, blustery house?" I asked them. Wrapped in blankets in my kitchen, feet on footstools, they were still wearing their wool hats and gloves, and looked as though they didn't know quite how to respond.

"My nearest neighbor is a mile away! What if I trip over Bracey and break my leg?"

"Don't worry," Nancy said, raising the earflaps on her husband's Gore-Tex hat. "In a few years, you'll be complaining about the new houses next door." She promptly lowered the flaps, and pulled the Hudson Bay blanket back up to her chin.

Settling in as best they could, the writers placed their notebooks on their laps and tried to write. They wrote about ardent dogs, night managers, nigella, solitary doves . . . Usually, they wrote until 11 a.m., at which point they'd stop and read their work aloud, if they wished. "Too many adverbs!" the group might respond. "What is the *story*?" "I like that word." "I hate that word." "Develop your characters." "It's perfect!" But today it was simply too cold. And so, after only a few minutes of polite conversation, clouds of steam hovering around their mouths, they said their goodbyes.

"This is my first real home," I said to Bracey after they'd gone, "*your* first real home—the first I've owned. But we can always return to New York. I've made no decision yet."

Bracey, lying on his bed, appeared stoic and composed, as always.

"I'm not the lesser person I used to feel in this house," I confide in him, "the foreigner." I talk to Bracey a lot, actually. "My identity is not my job, my work," I say. "I may be accustomed to plushy publishing offices and antiquey museum offices, but I can bone up on shoveling snow and feeding the woodstove." Bracey's ears flatten at the word *bone*; his eyes flicker with interest.

Before hauling the wood, say, or fetching the mail, I consult with Bracey. I also tell him about the opera we're hearing on the radio. Having listened all his life to the Saturday afternoon Metropolitan Opera broadcasts, he has, I think, acquired an appreciation of music. So he must expect such conversations, must want to know these things, and almost always pays full attention.

In our new life here, no matter what the temperature or season, Bracey and I have an evening ritual. Before we climb upstairs, we go outside for our bedtime walk. Unless it's raining—the only kind of weather he dislikes, thunder and lightning, especially—we circumnavigate the house slowly while he sniffs to see what creatures have been in the long grass and under the trees and along the driveway: it's his gossip column, his salt air society. And he will not be rushed in his pursuit of every last delicious tidbit. Occasionally, he halts in his tracks, ears pointed forward toward the blackness, a low growl in his throat. I beam my flashlight into the dark recesses of the woods, imagining murderers, assassins, but he continues his leisurely way, taking a whiff of dead iris and hosta, detouring to a patch of blackened monk's hood for a quick pee, absorbed, concentrated, a pro on the job.

This evening, halfway in our circuit, we stop at the wooden bench on the Point where there's a 180-degree view of the bay and the islands. Sometimes the moonlit view is as clear as in daylight, the islands low on the curved horizon, the water a silvery globe. Other times it's an impenetrable black, and only the noise of the surf signals the ocean's presence.

Threatened by the vast iciness of the waves, by their unseen expanse, I back off from this darkness, longing for New York and the bright, crowded streets of the Upper West Side, for the brassy tunefulness of French horns and the raucous blarings of taxi horns. But Bracey loves his walks here, including the winter ones. Willing to take risks, pad into the unknown, he's an eternal adventurer.

At night, when the full moon hangs over Eagle Island to the southwest, Bracey saunters through shadows cast on the frozen ground by spruce along the shore. The shadows look like animals

Bracey walks where I fear to

to me. Ambling across a fairly sinister camel, Bracey stops to snuffle the dried stalks of delphinium, blurring the crisp outline of the dromedary's face. These animals lie all around the house in the winter moonlight. Bracey and I have to watch our step. They are far bigger than Bracey. In fact, they consume him.

He makes his way to a bison, its shaggy, heavy chest dragging the snow-packed earth, then to a giant rabbit with great, long ears sitting in profile beside phantom hollyhocks, sweet peas, and ferns outlined in the snow. As we walk south, the moon sinks behind the trees, the shadows lengthen and deepen, and I almost stumble where the terrain suddenly darkens.

I look down, straight into nothingness. Bracey disappears, head first. I hear him mushing in the blackness. We are near the water. Could he have fallen over the bank?

I panic. "Bracey, where are you?" I call. "Come out! Quick!"

I can't see him in the drift of snow.

Little by little, I begin to discern images of trees emerging, as

Corgi angels in the snow

in a photographer's developing tray. More details issue: slender, two-inch spruce cones; long, slightly curved needles.

Finally, I see Bracey, walking where I fear to. He treads over a snow goose, steps on its large black wingtips.

"*Careful*, Bracey!"

I want to return to the house, put on a CD of *Der Fliegende Holländer*, stoke the woodstove, draw a hot bath; get into my flannel pajamas, my warm sheets, cover my head with blankets. Bracey is back with the giant rabbit, which has shifted its position, now facing me. I reach into its eyes to touch Bracey, his furry chest reassuring against my hand.

From the kitchen window the next morning, the sea looks closer, brought deceptively nearer by the new snow that fell in the night. All traces of our walk hours before are gone. The twisted trunks of spruces silhouetted against the water are black, the tall rust-colored grass under them a golden glow, the rugosa a shocking splash of yellow in the coldness. I let Bracey out into this scene. It's a winter palette, a winter Winslow Homer palette, authenticated by Bracey in his fox-red coat wriggling on his back, making corgi angels in the snow.

⇥ 8 ⇤

MELON SPOONS

A few days thereafter, I'm in the back of my bedroom closet looking for tax records I hid there last summer while tidying up for the renters. "We have to pay our estimated taxes, Bracey," I sigh, as I rummage through boxes of files. It's cold in the closet and the bedroom. Hardly any heat comes up through the floor register from the woodstove in the kitchen below. The stove probably needs stoking, in any case. Bracey, of course, is unaffected, his coat thick and warm. He lies comfortably on the floor by the bedroom door, dozing.

Among the cartons of documents, I come across a small, papier-mâché box from Kashmir. I'd brought it back with me after I visited my parents in Pakistan the summer of 1956 and traveled with them to Kashmir. In the box are letters from my mother and father, written shortly before my visit.

I take the box of letters down to the kitchen to read more carefully by the woodstove, which has almost totally cooled. Putting on my parka and wool hat, I tramp through the snow up to the woodshed next to the garage. Big-bellied gray clouds fill the sky; a few snowflakes fall. Bracey gleefully tries to catch them in his mouth. I haul a cartful of seasoned wood back to the house, carry several armfuls of it into the kitchen, and stack it neatly in a carrier next to the stove. Bracey shakes the snow off his coat and dances around me as I fill the stove with fresh logs. The kitchen smells of burning spruce and coffee. I settle down in the wicker chair next to the popping stove to read the letters.

"Now here is a little commission, if you can possibly manage it, from Mohammed, my faithful cook and friend," my mother wrote to me from Karachi.

He wants a small <u>round kitchen</u> spoon, like a little scoop, for making melon balls in a melon cocktail or also for small potatoes, the size of biggish marbles, made of any cheap material, purchased in any kitchen department or Woolworth's. . . . Mohammed would like two—and keeps asking daily if I have asked you! It really would make a hit at summer dinner parties to serve melon that way— something very new & different.

The other thing I wanted to say is: if you haven't got two cotton evening dresses one would be enough, as the social life of Karachi is closing down for the hot & monsoon season, alas. But don't let's worry—it will be such <u>heaven</u> to have you with us. Your loving, M."

Here's my mother concerned about melon balls and cotton evening dresses! But that was her job. She was happier, though, she noted, doing "a husky morning's work in my sick children's and babies' clinic in a terribly destitute refugee camp." She always took a deep interest in the problems of the people and country in which they lived. My father was the UN resident representative in Pakistan, concerned with the rehabilitation of refugees from the 1947 Partition, as well as water control, soil fertility, and the like. Jovial, friendly, an eminence in his international field, yet he couldn't help occasionally dropping names. He'd say, when he was with the State Department earlier in his career:

My dad, the Old China Hand, on vacation in Capri

"I had lunch with Adlai the other day, and he told me. . . ." Strange that I remember his saying he'd had lunch with Adlai but not what it was Adlai actually told him. Maybe all I needed was a daddy who lunched with Adlai or Ralph or Foster or Trygve! I find a letter to me in the box from my father, in which he wrote of their entertain-

My mother in my parents' Paris apartment

ing at a recent luncheon (without naming names, but we get the point): "a lady Pakistani tennis champion, the Pakistani Secretary of the Ministry of Refugees, an Australian UN expert on refugee housing, UK UN housing adviser, UK economic adviser. . . ." Embarrassing! But a bulwark, maybe, against his insecurities, his fears of failure, with which I now, alas, identify. "Work continues fascinating and challenging," he'd written a few months earlier. Then, too quickly: "Many top parties when the secretary general [at least he left out 'Dag'] was here. . . ." Did he think I wouldn't otherwise be interested in his work, which, so soon after the devastating Partition, was unquestionably demanding and exciting?

Under his influence, I'd always been politically active—beginning with my Milton Academy days. In front of the full Girls' School Assembly, I asked why there weren't any Jewish girls in the school. (I was called to the headmistress's office—certain I would be expelled—and told there hadn't been a sufficient number of applications.) When my father was pursued by the notorious House Un-American Activities Committee in 1949, I became further politicized. Home for the weekend from my sophomore year at Smith, a telegram arrived summoning him to appear before the

Committee. Our future was on hold for the next several days. The lives of many of my father's friends and colleagues who had answered the summonses and gone to Washington had been destroyed.

"I don't think I can send you back to Smith now," said my father, who was awaiting a State Department appointment. Then it occurred to him to call his old, if perhaps less than politically sympathetic, friend John Foster Dulles. "Don't go!" Dulles said. "The summons isn't legal. If they really want you, they'll subpoena you." So my father ignored the telegram, and I went back to college—and the rest is history. In fact, I've always been proud my father was a target of HUAC; that, as an Old China Hand, he didn't compromise his beliefs. He had taken care of himself.

In addition, my father made sure I accompanied him the following summer when he visited a large German family, the Kastls, friends of my parents, in Southern Bavaria. He was in Europe preparing for his State Department job with the Marshall Plan in Paris and I was headed for summer school in Grenoble before my Junior Year in Paris. The patriarch of the German family, Ludwig Kastl, had worked with my father at the League of Nations. During World War II, the Kastls had hidden Jewish families in their large chalet full of children, grandchildren, cats, dogs, and servants.

You'd never have known it, looking at those blond, blue-eyed beings at home in their warm, informal house, as I did just a few years after. Deep sofas in the salon and tennis rackets on the floor. No signs anywhere of what they'd done; no talk. Just one big, happy, ordinary family.

"Wollen zie haben die bratwurst und knödel?" Frau Kastl asked me as I sat down one evening at the dining table for *Abendessen*. The dining room window faced the distant Bavarian Alps. Two German shepherd dogs licked my ankles under the table. The noisily congenial family—about a dozen in all—passed bowls of steaming *salzkartoffeln* and platters of Wiener schnitzel and *weisswurst*, speaking half-German, half-English.

Kastl chalet in Southern Bavaria

(This was for my father's and my benefit, perhaps, although my father was fairly proficient in German, and I had a smattering: "Kann ich ein glasse weiss wein haben, bitte?"—words I'd learned at the first University of Vienna summer school held after the war in a castle on Lake Gmunden. There were no textbooks, only scores of Americans on the GI Bill—and *weinstubes* in the village nearby.)

"Ich liebe apfelstrudel!" I managed to say, as a granddaughter, dressed in a dirndl, set a plateful in front of me.

Had the Jewish families been sheltered in the cellar under my feet? I wondered. Or out in the barn with the cows? And how many were rescued in all? How were they brought out of Germany? I had so many questions. Yet, somehow, in this idyllic, serene family scene, I dared not ask them.

Kastl family with me kneeling

I've never forgotten the experience of visiting this family. In fact, its significance has become increasingly apparent to me in the years since.

My father also played his part, if small in comparison, by helping Dr. Frank, a German Jewish colleague, and his companion, Mrs. Bratz, to escape to the U.S. from Germany early in the war. For years, Dr. Frank and Mrs. Bratz, who settled in an apartment on Central Park South in New York, gave me thrillingly expensive Christmas and birthday presents—before I understood why.

Friendly and sweet, my father was far nicer, in many ways, than any of the Braces on my mother's side of the family. But he was hardly a superficial, party-sort-of guy. He worked hard and long. Nevertheless, he seemed to have needed more. I know. I recognize that need, or part of it. I never altogether believed my bosses when they praised my work, and always had to have additional confirmation.

Through a window facing west, I see, high in the sky, the smoky trail of a jet headed southwest, perhaps to New York City.

I invited my friend Varney—who, with her husband, Clint,

later visited me on Deer Isle and persuaded me to get a dog—to come with me on my trip to Pakistan and Kashmir. An attractive, reddish-blond-haired modern dancer and musician—her father was the composer Randall Thompson—Varney was always a delight to be with. She and I flew from New York to Karachi by propeller plane via Athens and Cairo, with a zigzag back across the Mediterranean to Beirut. It took nine days, with stopovers. Though scared of flying, I thrilled at descents over temples, mosques, and pyramids; paddy fields and plains. On our approach to Karachi, we circled above the seaport's surrounding beaches and cliffs on the Arabian Sea, swung low over its grand Anglo-Mughal state buildings and tall, shining minarets, cupolas, and arches.

Scanning the swarming, noisy Karachi airport, I picked out my father instantly. Over six feet tall, in a blue seersucker suit, he towered above the heads of the throngs about him, looking every bit the distinguished foreign diplomat in an exotic setting: handsome, cool, effective.

Mohammed and his colleagues

"Welcome, darling," my mother cried through the hubbub, hugging me and giving Varney a cordial handshake. In her flowered print dress, she appeared entirely unaffected by the blistering temperature.

"I've brought the spoons, Mummie!"

"Ah, Mohammed will be very happy," my mother said, giving me a kiss, her cheek cool and dry as it brushed mine.

9

HOOPOES' WINGS

In a dusty Chevrolet chauffeured by Jafar, a lanky, obliging young man, we drove into the city of Karachi along wide, bustling avenues teeming with men in white shirts and pajama trousers and women in burkhas. Camels hauled automobiles, steel girders, and towering piles of printed textiles in huge carts along the thoroughfares; their bells jingled and gonged. Brassware gleamed golden in little open-ended shops. The air was filled with the smells of cumin and turmeric.

My parents lived in Clifton, a residential area of large, old mansions and bungalows of the British Raj era—one- and two-story sandstone buildings and gardens enclosed by brick walls. Their house was an enormous, sprawling building, white with a red tile roof.

"Darling, let me show you and Varney our home," my mother said, "which I've spent much too much time decorating." She led us down marble corridors to drawing and sitting and dining rooms with pale green walls, to suites of bedrooms separated by mahogany, brass-knobbed doors, to the kitchen and servants' wing, which we did not enter. Elegant, print curtains stirred languidly in the stifling heat, barely moving under the ceiling fans. Peach-colored cushions cascaded over deep divans and cane chairs. Kashmiri prayer rugs covered tile floors. Everywhere, verandahs offered views of the lush, verdant garden and distant, aqua Arabian Sea.

"It's your grandest yet!" I said, utterly seduced, if displaced.

"Dreamy," Varney said.

With the box of my parents' letters scattered about me at my feet, I sit in a plain wicker chair in a simpler, smaller house now—

My parents' house in Clifton, a residential area of Karachi

not yet quite home, a little grand for me, and haunted by family ghosts. Recalling that Eastern sumptuousness, I look around at the workaday, wooden kitchen table and chairs and worn, braided rugs. Bracey paws at his L. L. Bean pillow, making a bed for himself. A home.

"I've found two nice young Pakistani students, Asad and Farid, for you and Varney to see the sights with," my mother said. "They're tall and handsome and can take you dancing in nightclubs. Not every night, of course. But occasionally. We want you with us, too."

Sure enough, in a couple of days, Asad and Farid came by and my mother introduced us. Asad thin, with black, lustrous hair; Farid long-legged, with a wide, generous forehead. Both of them studied economics at a private university in Karachi and spoke perfect American English. I fell for Asad instantly.

"We know how to jitterbug!" they told us, laughing, over cups of milky sweet tea. "We know how to be American!"

"Hooray!" Varney said.

"*I* don't even know how!" I said. So we went to clubs in which

Carrying a big load in Karachi

you could jitterbug and waltz, be American and Pakistani, or, rather, British colonial.

"Where can I eat the hottest possible curry?" I asked them one evening. "I like curry!"

"We'll try a working men's place downtown," Asad said.

And so, in a crowded basement cafeteria in the middle of the city, reeking of *tandoori* chicken and mutton *tikka* and filled with tables of men shoveling down curries, I had a small spoonful of a curry called *Karahi*. I was instantly on fire, a flaming torch. Nothing helped—not a glass of water, not yogurt.

"I'd never try curry here myself," Farid said, grinning.

"I won't, either!" Varney said

Sweat poured down my chin, dripped onto my ruby-red nylon skirt.

"It's all right," I said. "I love it, I really do."

And I still do.

"We've planned a holiday in Kashmir," my father said at breakfast one morning in the smaller of the two dining rooms, overlook-

A busy street in the heart of Karachi

ing a grove of coconut palm trees, in their house. We were eating cheese omelets with hot, crunchy puri buns, chick-peas, mangoes, and honey. "I want you to eat Pakistani food," my mother had said. "Too many Americans here buy food at the PX. Such a pity." She poured chai from a glazed, fern-green teapot into light yellow teacups.

"We've rented a houseboat on Dal Lake," my father said amiably, sipping his tea.

"You and Varney must come with us,"

Mohammed, lean-limbed, with fine, long fingers, wearing a brown shirt and white pajama trousers, came in from the kitchen wing.

"How you enjoy your breakfasts?" he asked.

"I adore your *puris*," I said shyly.

"Plenty good enough," he nodded.

A week later, we flew to Delhi.

We couldn't get to the Indian part of Kashmir directly from Pakistan. Relations between the two countries since the bloody

1947 Partition were dangerously tense. Moreover, India was dubious about all the Americans in Pakistan, particularly highly visible officials such as my father. In addition to the UN assistance, Pakistan was receiving millions of dollars in military and economic aid from the U.S.

In the mahogany bar of our hotel in Delhi that evening, a Dutch tourist told us there had been several plane accidents during the past year in the pass into Kashmir.

"Ogh, you know, so many people have been killed, so many bodies found on rough, sharp peaks and pieces of plane on short branches."

My father offered the blue-eyed Dutchman a drink. Sipping gins and tonic—my mother required something stronger, a martini—we listened to his account. Planes were required to fly with full visibility, he said—no instrument flights allowed. We raised our glasses prayerfully to Air India.

From Delhi, we flew to a small, dusty airport—an outpost for flights north through the Pir Panjal Mountains—in the middle of a pebbly desert in northwestern India. There, waiting on the earthen runway, was a tiny Air India propeller plane, and we filed into it with five other passengers. My parents sat in front of Varney and me, two rows from the door to the pilot's cockpit.

As we took our seats, my mother snapped her alligator purse open and shut. Always terrified of flying, she'd been a wreck on our flight here. Even in the relatively large Pakistan Airways and Air India planes, she'd been restive and fidgety. Now her head shook badly as the plane headed down the runway, rose in the air for a few minutes, before abruptly—and sickeningly—dropping back to the ground and bumping to a stop.

Oh, my God! I looked at Varney and attempted to smile.

Behind me, an English passenger chortled and said, "Pilot forgot his toothbrush!" My mother's head was now quivering uncontrollably.

We taxied back to the airport's shoddy structures, where a man in a shapeless business suit and sandals told us to get out.

"What happened?" my mother cried, climbing down the rickety steps drawn up to the cabin door. "Why are we doing this?"

"Maybe the pilot didn't put enough gas in the plane," my father joked. He held her hand as we watched the plane refuel (at the very least, one assumed, to replace what had just been used for liftoff). Directed to a low shed, we were offered bottled fruit juice. I drank the sweet liquid directly from the bottle, my hand trembling.

Soon, the man in the business suit, saying something about a "remedied mechanic failure," signaled us to return to the plane. We crossed the runway back to the plane's steps. My mother's face turned bright red and she began to perspire heavily.

"I won't get back in," she said.

"What else can we do?" my father said, laying his hand lightly in the small of her back.

"The plane will crash, you'll see!" she cried.

"Oh, Mummie," I said, "It's our only way out." A collapsing figure, my mother stumbled onto the plane, gripping my father's arm. Again, we taxied unevenly down the sandy runway and became airborne, the plane dipping its wings over the flat, red terrain. Ahead of us enormous clouds, churned into spiraling, ballooning spheres, hid the mountains.

The co-pilot, wearing a turban and mufti, came out of the cockpit and stood at the front of the cabin. His eyes were deep set, his lips full. He spoke English with care.

"We must fly with vision," he said. "See these clouds?" he gestured toward the portholes. "We must pass through them intelligently. We must see light and air. It is not recommended to penetrate them blindly." He returned to the cockpit.

The plane approached the first tower of clouds, circled for several minutes, darted up through a hole into a higher level of stratosphere, circled and darted again. From my seat next to the window, I watched apprehensively as we executed these stomach-heaving gyrations. Varney, calmer and braver, distracted herself with a book of Yeats's poetry. The plane repeated these movements for close to an hour, long enough that I began to search for the openings in the clouds myself in order to brace for the sudden, upward spirals.

Emerging from the cockpit, the co-pilot stood once again at the front of the cabin: "We have obtained sufficient heights to navigate the pass," he said. "We see almost properly." Puffs of translucent clouds trailed around the plane, occasionally veiling the angular, bare peaks of purplish gray stone on either side of us, which our wings appeared nearly close enough to touch. Far below us, a serpentine trail wound through the pass—over which camels and nomads carried supplies from India and the outside world—darkened by the slowly creeping shadow of the plane.

I tried to enjoy the view, as I knew my mother couldn't. She'd flown throughout the Belgian Congo, under similar scenic circumstances, she'd told me, continuously tortured by fear. Probably, as she stared out the porthole, she imagined the plane diving into the pass, knocking its wings on the sides of the mountains as it went down, smashing the camels and nomads as it hit the ground.

And suddenly, such portents were borne out: the plane plunged straight down! Suitcases and golf clubs spilled out of the overhead compartments, plates and glasses from the galley rolled down the floor under our feet toward the cockpit.

This was the end. I'd seen it in movies. The passengers scream and scream and hold onto each other and then it's all over.

I don't know whether I screamed, but I clung to Varney tightly. She clutched my arm, her green eyes wide and frantic. She knew it as well as I did: We were going to die.

But then, as swiftly as it had begun plummeting, the plane straightened out, and we were level again. I was in a debris of open cases: a yellow-and-mauve print nylon dress hung over my left shoulder, a white slip trailed around my neck. Varney was encased in a billowing, ivy-green sari. A plate of curried squid squelched on the floor under my sandals. Mushy yellow dal oozed under our seats. The sun shone into the topsy-turvy cabin, onto the traumatized, dumbstruck survivors. We were totally undone. Except for my mother!

"I told you so," she said triumphantly. "I *told* you we were all going to die."

Her cheeks were pink, her eyes reflecting the brilliant, opalescent Kashmir sky. She looked positively radiant.

"Sorry, sorry, my apologies," said the co-pilot, reappearing now from the cockpit, his turban impeccably in place. "We sight a buzzard, he is in a pattern right on target for our windshields or engines. Unwise not to pay attention or predict his very activities and so must philosophize his movements until the absolute moment he is within adequate centimeters of our fuselage. We wait and before inevitable collision, downward take passage. Very dangerous otherwise, cognizant subterfuge on our part, but apologies for disturbance."

My father, true, fearless flier, was still pale. Wiping sweat from his brow, however, he managed to speak: "You are to be congratulated, sir. In all my flights over the Alps, across the Pacific, into Africa, I've never experienced an avoidance dive so well executed as this. Please extend my compliments to the pilot."

We slumped back in our seats, exhausted—*kofta* kabobs bobbing among *puris* on the cabin's floor—until we descended at last into the Vale of Kashmir, Jehangir's Garden of Eternal Spring, to the shining, ancient city of Srinagar. The plane at last coming to a halt on the tarmac, my mother gathered her purse and, before exiting the plane, walked two rows forward to retrieve her straw hat from under a seat. Smiling, the hat now perched at a fetching angle, she looked like a young girl at a seaside picnic in Maine.

At customs, in the airport at Srinagar, glad to be on terra firma, we nevertheless handed over our passports a little uneasily. My father had mentioned before we left Karachi there was the remote chance, given their resentment of his role in Pakistan, the Indian authorities might decide to hold us when the time came to leave. But our good fortune persisted and there was no problem.

A cart, called a *tonga*—with two big wooden wheels and a tilted canvas canopy—was sent to meet us at the airport by our landlord, Rahim, the owner of the houseboat we would be occupying. Drawn by a pony, it conveyed us bumpily through Srinagar. We passed steepled, pagoda-like wooden mosques and labyrinths of alleyways and bridges over the Jhelum River, which threaded its way through the city. My mother, full of energy, radiated appreciation for the intricately carved wooden shrines. "Sahibs, Sahibs!" called out the street hawkers, showing their wares. "See shawls, admire carpets, obtain massages!"

Out of the city, on our way to Dal Lake, we beheld the Himalayas to the north. Seeming to spring directly out of the valley's ninety miles of extravagantly fertile soil, the snow-capped mountains towered over hemp and saffron fields, rice paddies, and apple and apricot orchards.

Now, with Bracey close by in his bed, I scratch his ears and observe, through the kitchen window, the Camden Hills, their soft, rounded tops strung along the southwestern perimeter of the bay. So much smaller—so much more comforting—than the Himalayas, yet also majestic from this distance. My Camden Himalayas.

At Dal Lake, Rahim, clean shaven, in a dark suit and fez, greeted us with two large, gondola-like, taxi *shikaras*. Ordering the boatmen to load our luggage in the first, he escorted us aboard the second, which had a straw-covered wooden roof and blue curtains. We reclined on scarlet and plum cushions imbedded with small mirrors and trimmed with gold tassels. Finally, I allowed myself to relax among the pillows. Our two *shikara wallahs*—one with a white turban, the other a black skull cap—propelled us smoothly with their heart-shaped paddles across the two-and-a-half-mile-wide by five-mile-long lake; the fringed curtains fluttered as we moved forward.

Lotus and water lilies crowded our path across the lake; melting sounds of ragas, sung by boat people, who ferried goats and hay and vegetables in their *shikaras*, skimmed the water, glanced off the houseboats moored nose-to-stern, like carved elephants on an ivory bracelet, around the lake's western edge. The lower slopes of the silver-peaked Himalayas, replicated in the still water, started to turn purplescent in the lengthening day. Masses of roses grew among running streams and fountains in the terraced Mughal gardens on the shore. The heavy, sweet scents of honeysuckle and wild white dog roses followed our passage. Tall, straight poplars and smaller willows stood at attention.

"Look, a kingfisher!" Varney cried, pointing at a flash of blue and green among the willows.

"Kingfishers here by hundreds," Rahim said, smiling. "Listen." Sure enough, we could hear their raucous cries all through the treetops. "Also bulbuls, hoopoes, doves, flycatchers," he counted on his fingers. "You will learn to see them."

The *shikara wallahs*, with Rahim guiding them, paddled us to our houseboat, a massive wooden structure moored by chains to great pegs driven into the bank. The houseboat had elaborate,

Our houseboat seen behind the *shikara wallahs*

Himalayas from Dal Lake

sculpted carved cedar verandahs and windows, over which hung scalloped white awnings.

"How grand, how majestic she is!" my mother laughed, still refreshed by vindication. "Except for her name—'Dunrovin.' But isn't that typically British!"

Built during the Victorian era for the British colonial administrators, who were forbidden by the maharajas to buy land, the houseboats came to function as grand vacation homes.

We climbed the ornamental stairway to her stern, shaded by a wooden canopy and filled with yet more colorful cushions and faded oriental rugs. Everything was alluring and luxurious—all the more so for being a little worn. I was thrilled and overwhelmed—and totally isolated, even with my parents there. And Varney, too. I was the child. Separate. Alongside. But alone.

Varney and I followed my parents down the hallway to the various spacious rooms. The living room had an ornate cedar-paneled ceiling and an abundance of Bokhara rugs; the dining room, a

My parents in a *shikara*, our houseboat in the background

hand-carved walnut table and matching chairs. "Wowee, that's one huge chandelier," Varney said, pointing to the elaborate brass fixture suspended over the dining table. The three bedrooms, each with a bathroom, glowed with embroidered curtains and bedspreads. Victorian Mughal. Heavy and ornate.

A cook boat with the kitchen and staff was hitched to the bank next to the houseboat. At mealtimes, the waiter walked along the shore with steaming dishes and entered our boat by a plank. He brought us pomegranate lamb, dal with chili peppers, saffron tripe garnished with tulips, serving it with a bow. All I could think of was Blanche's fried haddock back on Deer Isle, of her shouting from the kitchen, "Are you ready for the fish?" What a contrast. She'd never have put up with all this fuss.

Most of the windows in the houseboat faced the lake, which was endlessly trafficked by elderly, turbaned men with white beards offering massages, women in cotton saris selling cucumbers and melons, tomatoes and lotus. They'd paddle their *shikaras*

Flower sellers alongside the houseboat

right under our windows to hold up papier-mâché boxes and bunches of zinnia and cosmos.

At breakfast the next day, Varney said, "I think I'll play my flute on the top deck." We mounted the outer stairs to the tent on the upper deck. She played the Air on the G String by Bach and an adaptation of a melody from her father's choral work *Alleluia* (which I recently sang, with much joy and connection, with the Deer Isle Congregational Church choir). Her notes floated out to join the boatmen's songs, soft splashes of heart-shaped paddles, and whispery beatings of hoopoes' wings. The last alleluias slipped among the lotus blossoms.

With a happy sigh, Varney took out pen and paper from her pocket, the shadowed Himalayas in the distance framing her shining red hair. "I'm going to write a letter to Clint," she said. Clint, her fiancé, was a composer, like her father. He was in Greece for the summer.

I gazed down on a Kashmiri woman, her long head scarf trailing down her back, as she paddled by in a skiff filled to the brim with feathery weeds from the lake's edges. It was paradise. A lonely paradise. I wished I had a fiancé to write to. But all I'd left behind me was a tangle of half-developed relationships.

"Perhaps you and Varney might like to take a *shikara* to the houseboat in the middle of the lake," my father said at lunch, after finishing off a mutton *seekh* kabob, one of several on his plate. "It used to be a British club for eating, dancing, and swimming."

There, a bespectacled Indian taught us to water ski—a ridiculous way to spend time in a place like Kashmir, but why not, we thought, as it seemed to be the principal recreation on the lake. People didn't water ski on Penobscot Bay. Not in my family, anyway—the water too cold, the sport not serious. A little tacky even.

Two small speedboats whisked Varney and me all across Dal Lake, spray from their wakes obliterating the view of the exotic surroundings. I fell over a few times at first, lost hold of the rope, endured tiny moments of anxiety in the chilly water, waiting for my boat man to come back and throw me the line to pull me back up on my feet. Eventually, I stayed up for fifteen minutes, then half an hour. I whirled around and around the northern part of the great lake, where there were fewer lily pads. Mountains and trees and bright foliage passed in wide, precarious sweeps, reminding me of my skating figure eights as a child in Switzerland.

In this way, Varney and I met Jock, a Scottish UN peacekeeping trooper, and Alan, the British pilot of the UN plane, who were spending their leaves on Dal Lake. Slim, of medium height, with a fine, straight nose, Alan flew the big, blue UN plane in and out of Kashmir. Crossing borders forbidden to all but him, he policed thousands of dangerous miles between the Pakistani and Indian portions of Kashmir.

Alan, pilot of the UN plane

"Will you teach me how to water ski properly?" I asked him one afternoon as we sat together in our bathing suits on the top deck of the houseboat club.

"Why not?" he said, moving a little closer.

"You mean you water skied, you wasted your time

Varney, Jock, me, and Alan at an old British colonial club in Srinagar

getting wet and bothered behind a motor boat in Kashmir, for heaven's sake?" Eleanor said the following summer at Deer Isle, when I told her about my adventures. "What were your parents doing?" Reading, I expected, lounging among the tasseled cushions. Enjoying themselves.

Varney and I played golf with Alan and Jock at Gulmarg, on top of a mountain: the highest golf course in the world, another former British club. "The Indians find it very satisfactory to use the British colonial recreational facilities," Alan said with relish, nodding his blond head. "I can understand. Those insufferable *pukka sahibs*, those ghosts . . ."

Climbing up and down flower-carpeted meadows—with colossal views of Nanga Parbat—we followed our golf balls to immaculate greens that floated in milky air, suspended from the sides of the pine- and fir-covered mountain.

I didn't tell Eleanor about this. She thought it was silly to play golf on Deer Isle, let alone halfway across the world in a paradise one would see only once.

In Srinagar, we danced at an old British club whose French doors opened onto a white-blooming garden of orchids. I felt safe and cherished in the strong arms of my pilot. One evening, Alan and I took a *shikara* alone together back to the houseboat. As we kissed among the pillows, stretched out on the full-length, sofa-like space, entwined under the Kashmiri stars and moon, he proposed to me.

More than a little intrigued and attracted by this romantic hero, I tried to imagine life with a UN pilot. Pictured myself on borders in Bhutan and Tibet, practicing a colonial life in remote mountains or desert compounds, eating curries made from ingredients purchased at the PX. It was not such a very farfetched idea; indeed, would not have been so different from my life until then, which had been spent ricocheting back and forth between Europe and the U.S.

On the top deck of the houseboat club where we water skied

Terrified of being alone for the rest of my life, equally terrified of being trapped, I was a wanderer, searching for homeport but reluctant to tie up, almost comfortable in my anxiety, leery of permanent rejection and permanent connections alike. For now, though, I let myself be courted in this exotic, fluid realm, although ultimately I would say no.

One night at 3 a.m., my mother's and father's voices broke through the single layer of paneling that stood between my room and theirs. I awoke, annoyed. I needed my sleep for water skiing and golfing; for necking with my pilot in the moonlight.

My mother's voice grew louder. I got up, walked along the corridor to their room and tapped on the door.

"What's the matter?" I said, entering the room.

My father lay in bed, arms at his sides, beads of perspiration on his forehead.

"Your father isn't feeling well," my mother said, flustered. His breathing was clearly labored. "He may be having a heart attack." She looked at me with what seemed almost hostility and blame. Instantly, I was undone.

"Oh, God, Mummie, what can we do?" I cried. I lurched over to his bed, touched his rigid arm. "Will you be all right?" I said.

"I'll be fine, Bren," my father whispered. I squeezed his hand.

"What can we do?" I repeated.

"Well, he's a little better already," my mother said. "The worst is over, I think." She adjusted the sheet over his chest. Her medical expertise had taken over. The houseboat rocked gently. "We'll wait and call a doctor tomorrow."

At that moment, Varney came to the door. "Is something wrong?" she said.

"Daddy's sick," I said. "Mummie thinks he may have had a heart attack."

"How terrible!" Varney said, stepping back in shock. "I'm so sorry!"

"Go back to bed, girls," my mother said. "Leave us now."

Varney gave my mother a hug and bent down to murmur a word to my father before she returned to her room.

"He's *got* to be all right, Mummie," I said. I tried to be strong, not to cry. I squeezed my mother's shoulders. She let me hold her for a few seconds. "Go on to bed, dear," she said. I leaned down to kiss my father on his cheek.

"I'll be on the verandah for a little while," I said. "I can't sleep."

And so I sat out in the moonlight, leaning against the mirrored cushions. Icy filaments, caught by moonbeams, blinked and glistered along the tops of the mountains. I had no right to be in this paradise, to romance my pilot—to spend so little time with my parents. My mother had told me just the day before how inconsiderate I was, enjoying myself too much with the peacekeepers. Told me the reason she and my father had invited me on this trip was (in part) to keep them company. "Your father desires your attention," she said. Had she pushed me in this direction before, toward this reluctant sort of intimacy?

"You're selfish," she said.

She'd said much the same, of course, in London, New York, Paris, Brussels: I felt by now as if the words had been embossed in satiny, raised letters on a black ribbon that wrapped my throat and fingers, entwined my feet. I was unworthy to help in crises—in this one or any other. These were my thoughts on the verandah in the moonlight.

Here in the Deer Isle house, with my parents' letters scattered on the floor, it occurs to me perhaps I hadn't been the one who was selfish. I'd been a diversion, after all. On call. My family role.

Bracey has moved from his bed and lies with his nose on my shoes. Across the bay, the Camden Hills press bluely into the clouded, broken sky.

The following morning, I recollect, a doctor came across the lake from Srinagar.

"Heart attack," he pronounced, "but unexcessive. He must repose easy, in light of which he will recuperate very fine."

"Your father is getting better, dear," my mother said a few days later. "So you and Varney can still do the trek in the Himalayas we planned for you. Abdullah will lead you. We'll stay here on the houseboat. Don't worry about us."

On the eve of our departure, however, I contracted a fever of 103 degrees and chills. We debated whether to cancel the trip. "Go!" my mother said, with uncharacteristic vigor. "When will you ever have another chance? Hang onto your pony—he'll get you up the first mountain. Then you can rest. Abdullah will take Varney fishing until you regain your strength." She had it all worked out.

Climbing the lower slopes of the Himalayas

The next day, as trees gave way to boulders and forty-five-degree solid-rock inclines, I held on to my mountain pony, one of six on the expedition. Sweating and feverish, almost sliding off several times, my legs were splayed across the pony, dangling like a soft puppet's, feet brushing glacial lichen and pointed rocks. I willed my arms to stay around the pony's neck as I slipped back toward her rump.

To the side of the path was a drop of several hundred feet. I was horrified when one of the ponies—thankfully, carrying rugs and pots and pans, not a sharp-edged cot—fell off the trail and rolled down the mountainside into a crevice. The seven bearers, with rags tied together for shoes, clambered down the incline to where the pony lay, neighing and whinnying, eyes rolling in fear, and hauled him and his burden up with their bare hands.

"Let's go back," I wanted to cry to Abdullah and Varney. "I'm ill and scared." But I stayed quiet, stroked my pony's mane, aromatic of grass, and murmured words of encouragement to her.

Our tent

At our first campsite, on a glacial lake high in the Himalayas, I had to be helped off my pony by two of the bearers, who were kindly and good-natured. Abdullah then directed all the bearers to raise our tent. With much noise and enthusiastic shouting, they erected two layers of canvas supported by two poles. Embellished with scalloped edges, the outer layer provided additional protection from the sun and rain. An alcove, formed by a semicircular flap on the inside, held a chamber pot and a bowl for washing. Two cots, a bedside table, and felt rugs furnished the tent itself. I passed out on one of the cots and slept for twenty-four hours, waking occasionally to sip water and East India tea.

The first day, Abdullah and Varney fished for trout on the shores of the lake. Through the open tent flap, I saw the glacier reflected behind their figures, the snowy mountain peaks behind the glacier, a buildup of images on a blue metal disc: from ordinary clay to plunging, icy debris to soaring certitudes.

The next day, I was well enough so we could continue our trip.

Picnic

Varney and I rode our surefooted ponies, while Abdullah walked close by. The bearers and load-ponies followed. "You will see, plenty of trout at next lake," Abdullah said. "But it's the *mountains* we want to see," we cried. Somehow we always reached a compromise: a lake full of fish at the foot of a mountain or by a glacier. Up and down the mountainsides we climbed—through woodlands and along torrential streams, across high pastures and grasslands smelling of clover, and beside lavender glaciers. We camped in meadows with velvety soft grass and tall forget-me-nots and on stony, yellow-brown slopes. Woolly clouds drifted above us, folding in on the peaks.

At a different campsite every evening, Varney and I sat in front of our tent in upright wooden chairs at a small folding dining table set with glasses and silverware on a pale green cloth. We could smell meat cooking on the fire built by the bearers near their tent, pitched less than a hundred feet from ours. The bearers talked and laughed as they cooked *roganjosh* (meat with spices), which they brought and served to us on a platter beneath the luminous Himalayan peaks.

Even as Varney and I tried to speak of what we had seen and done—and of where we were and where we would be the next day . . . and after—the mountains stopped us. Made everything seem footling, inconsequential.

"I can't believe this," Varney said one evening, sipping her chai. "It's not happening." Above us, a mountain peak shot crimson bolts into the opalescent sky.

"And yet it's all true!" I said. "It *is* happening."

From time to time, tribes of nomadic shepherds, Gujars, would pass us, bells on their wrists, on their cattle and goats. Barefoot, the men were in *pherans* (a blend of coat and cloak) and white turbans; the women in wonderful, wide trousers, with babies on their backs wrapped in shawls. Silver ornaments spangled at their necks. The Gujars drove their flocks with wild, shrill hawk-whistles. They were the only people we saw.

The last day of the trek, from a lofty ridge above the Vale of Kashmir, we gazed at circle upon circle of mountains stretched around the entire horizon. Slowly, we descended to fir and oak, to *chinar* and poplar and willow, to carpets of ferns and flowering grasses, to lucent water.

"We're back," I called, as I jumped onto the stern of the houseboat. My mother came out to the deck from the living room. "Oh, we had such a *fantastically* marvelous time!" I said.

"Goodness me, you've returned looking ever so much better!" she said, looking startled. And a little aggrieved?

I run my fingers over Bracey's muzzle. He raises his head and peers at me with a bright, sprightly expression. "Hey, I showed a *little* gumption there, don't'ya think, Bracey, love?"

✦ 10 ✦

MY UFFIZI

In mid-December, I ask a carpenter-friend, Gary, to insulate part of the house to form a warm space for Bracey and me, a house-within-a-house. I've been reluctant until now to change a thing.

Perhaps if I start small . . .

I decide to begin with my bedroom, study, and bathroom at the north end. Gary frames in the outside walls and inserts three-and-a-half-inch fiberglass batting; then he tapes and muds. Tess, his wife, paints the bathroom pale blue with dark blue splashes: the wall behind the tub, the slanted beam, and the antique, wooden water tank six feet overhead from which the toilet is flushed with a chain.

With his fur coat, Bracey's not aware that we've been living under arctic conditions. And his position inside the sunny front door, from which he surveys the exterior world of crows, gulls, and squirrels, is secure. He's entirely untroubled. But islanders are taking bets on how long we can last.

Roman, Gary and Tess's large, gentle dog—part wolf—accompanies them to work. Bracey and Roman play among the rolls of fiberglass and coils of tape. I worry they'll eat the fiberglass. I also worry about a wolf amusing himself with my corgi.

"Oh, don't worry—he's a living doll," Gary says. "Bought him from a guy who breeds them. Swore he wouldn't hurt a baby."

Gary's up on a ladder in the tiny study, plastering the ceiling overhead, his long brown hair well-spattered with white. Through the dormer window, I see Roman bounding and leaping in the snow with Bracey. He looks back at his short-legged friend, slowing down to let him catch up.

"Such a gentleman," I say.

Then he flattens his shaggy torso on the snow in play and Bracey goes nose-to-nose with him.

"I think Bracey's in love with Roman," I say. "And with you, too, Gary," I add.

Each morning, when Gary arrives at the house, he sits on the floor with Bracey, cradles him in his arms, invites kisses. An expression of rapture spreads over Bracey's face, brown eyes half-closed in enchantment, black nostrils shining.

With a little heat from the woodstove in the kitchen rising through the new register Gary's put in to help warm my bedroom, it's becoming habitable upstairs. I begin to dream of constructing a small, insulated addition, of making at least this end of the building a year-round house. But is this heresy, to tamper with Longfellow's original design?

At a party toward the end of December, I meet Don, an architect from New York, who has just moved to the island year round with his wife, Ginger, also an architect. "Do the drawings yourself," he says. "I'll critique them."

For two weeks, I dither. I stew. I can't possibly produce drawings fit for Don's distinguished eyes. And do I really want to live year round in this forsaken back of beyond, anyway?

However, working with an engineer's ruler and furniture templates, I manage to make a few drawings on graph paper. Bracey remains calm, but curious, as I crawl across the floor to do my measurements. He supposes I'm down there to romp, though I hardly seem very sportive.

In a frenzy of dreaming, I sketch dozens of plans and variations: I glass in the small screened porch under my bedroom on the north end of the house facing the water; extend the pantry six feet on the eastern side; add nine feet to the kitchen to the north. Timorously, I take my portfolio of drawings to Don.

He discards all but a drawing of the addition to the north. After which, using a heavy pencil on tracing paper, he widens and expands the kitchen eighteen by thirty feet to incorporate a small

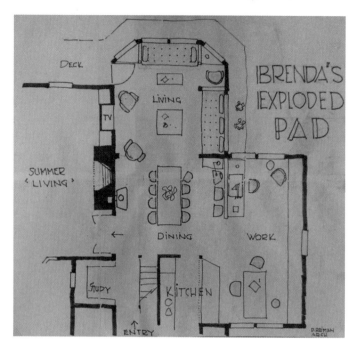

Don Reiman's drawing of the addition to the north,
and the later addition to the west with the bay window

sitting area with sofa and chairs, a dining table, and shelves for books and bibelots.

"But . . ." I begin. My heart is thumping.

And it's done. The first of Don's many divine drawings of my addition.

"The floors will be warmer," I reassure Bracey on our way home. "We will have new yellow pine floors."

None of this can happen until May, however—until the snow melts, the ground has softened, and Gary can get back to work on the house.

Bracey and I spend these months huddled by the woodstove, during which I shilly-shally.

"Do we honestly want to dwell on this lonesome, cold peninsula?" I say to him. He looks bored. He hears the same refrain, day and night.

I do, however, buy a big gas cookstove-cum-heater and have it installed in the kitchen, where it provides more regular heat, and move the woodstove up to my bedroom.

In the meantime, three raccoons and four squirrels have taken over my garage. Out for a free fix whenever they can get it, the raccoons have noticed I keep sunflower seeds for my birdfeeder in large garbage pails in the garage and make an easy job of removing the lids before going to sleep for the winter. So Gary, who continues to do small tasks around the property, observed carefully by Bracey and Roman, builds a lockable bin for the pails, which he gradually improves upon over the winter. First he places a heavy countertop, with bolts at each end, over the three plastic pails, figuring that way the raccoons can't pull the lids off. The squirrels, however, eat right through the plastic. So he adds a plywood front and substitutes metal pails for the plastic. Joined in early spring by the awakening raccoons, the squirrels find a way through a gap at the back of the improvised bin. They get the lids off by chewing through the crisscrossed bungee cords and sliding the lids sideways under the countertop.

On an icy brilliant March morning, I lift the countertop to see a raccoon sitting in one of the garbage pails, his delicate hands plastering his mouth with seeds. Cushioned on the soft, shifting riches of black and gray striped seeds, he seems almost drowsy from the plenty, his eyes milky with satisfaction. He's on a binge inside a tin can, seeds cascading underneath him, spilling downhill as he moves his soft bottom from one side to the other or reaches deep into the pebbly mix with his elongated, Dürer-like fingers. I quickly slam the countertop down again. Mercy!

Gary plugs the hole behind the bin and puts metal chains on the garbage pail lids. Of course, these are nearly as hard for me to unhook as they are for the damn animals, and in my struggles to get at the birdseed, I skin my fingers in the cold temperatures, cursing these interlopers.

At least, I've found a way to outsmart the squirrels at the delivery end, I think, rigging up a foolproof, fail-safe pulley system for the birdfeeder on a birch tree trunk.

But in late spring, once the raccoons really get going, I'm proved wrong. One evening, the female unhooks the line leading to the birdfeeder from the screw eye on the tree trunk and lowers it by pulley to the ground. Tucking into my customary mixture of raisin bran and Cheerios the next morning, I see the feeder through the kitchen window: prone in the grass, lid askew, empty.

"It's a rummy rig," I spit out angrily, slopping hot decaf over my ravaged hands. The instant I open the front door, Bracey races over to inspect the devastation.

This time, I belay the hook with copious rounds of picture wire to the screw eye on the tree trunk. "See if you can cast loose *that* line," I shout into the trees along the driveway. Bracey barks with excitement. In bed that night, I take a certain amount of pleasure in imagining the animals' fury at being stymied. Bracey's paws jerk beside me in some dream or nightmare.

At daybreak, I rush to the window. Picture wire shines in great loops amidst the dandelions and mustard plants under the birdfeeder, the hook at the end of the wire to the screw eye popped, and the feeder again barren.

Abandoning the pulley system, I hang the feeder instead from the middle of a long wire strung between two birches. I hunker down to watch, as if vigilance alone might keep the raccoons from winning. But it is not to be. Balancing himself on the line that evening, partially illuminated by the light from the house, Philippe Petit, crown prince of tightrope walkers, reaches down and releases the hook easily enough from the top of the feeder. Seeds spray in the air, spreading like grain from a silo. While, underneath the wire, three fat raccoons sit together like the Fates, munching, munching, munching . . .

The daffodils arrive, and with them, Gary to his full-time renovation work on the big house. He slices lumber with screeching machines. Bracey observes unflinchingly. Posts are poured; old bead board stripped; two-by-four studs and floor and ceiling joists are installed. Bracey's vigilant through it all. As new cedar shingles are nailed to the sides and roof of the house, he patrols the perimeter, listening to Don and Gary talk of soffits and fascias and flashing. With Gary and Roman back, it is clear, life is good. Bracey follows them everywhere.

I invite all the plumbers, electricians, painters, and cabinet-makers to bring their dogs to work. Carol has her mutt and a golden; Jay, her poodle mix; Tony, his hound. It's dog heaven. One day I count seven dogs. Bracey, delighted, reigns supreme.

Once in a while, he goes too far, however, and starts to herd his friends, forgetting what happened in Central Park when, after he tried herding the dogs in his playgroup, they turned on him and snapped. Deluded into thinking he was consequential and had a duty to perform, that nothing must divert him from his task, he simply barked louder and louder that day, the better to do the job. Hush! cried the dog owners, but he couldn't stop himself. Only after all the dogs, followed by their mistresses and masters, had fled to their apartment buildings, did he look around and see what he had done. His officiousness had driven them away.

This time, the dogs don't run off, but remain rooted to the Maine earth, snarling at his oafishness.

"It's a trade-off, Bracey," I tell him "Either you keep them as pals or treat them like cattle. But you can't do both."

I have my own choices to make, as well, although of a different order.

"Do you want fine cherry-wood edging on the cabinet tops?" asks Don, offering Bracey a biscuit. "Do you think three electric outlets next to the kitchen peninsula are sufficient? And maybe four at the foot of the stairs?" asks Sonny, the electrician, stroking Bracey's tummy with his powerhouse hands. "Do you wish to keep the old, wooden toilet in the upstairs bathroom?" asks Tony, the plumber, patting Bracey on his rear.

New addition, awash in reflected sea light

Each of these questions sends me into a frenzy of uncertainty.

On occasion, I imagine my family ghosts whispering among themselves, floating in the bridged ceiling. They circle endlessly, regarding me with seduction and witchery. They evaluate every minute of my day—I'm building a home onto theirs, you see—and they monitor my interior passage to a new life. Their breath fills their part of the house, hangs over the Morris chairs and rattan sofa like rain clouds over the Jungfrau.

I gaze back at them from my end—with its shiny kitchen and expansive living area—through the mahogany doors, between new and old, protected by the invisible scrim.

Slowly, my fixers, Don and the builders of my dream, create a magic box where I can live in beauty and solitude. Walls are extended, with shelves built on the long, north wall; a yellow pine floor is installed, with latitude for seating and dining. The sea fills the big glass windowpanes to the brim, lighting the whole space, the room awash in reflected sea light, a creamy blue aquarium of riches.

Ghosts' view of addition through the mahogany doors

One Saturday afternoon, I lie on the floor of the addition, weeping as I listen to the Met broadcast of *Lohengrin*, homesick for the Opera House, for New York. Bracey, next to me, licks my wet cheeks. I raise myself to look out the windows at the most beautiful prospect in the world.

Nor is the work over yet. Bracey, setting aside his herding failures, delights in the company of dogs. I'm gaining in confidence, too, thriving on the new growing out of the old like a flower blossoming off of a woody, old stem. Somehow, I learn to sing back to my family ghosts: I'm composing an enchanted life in my room awash in sea grays and music greens.

I even summon the courage to ask Gary to restore the loggia on the front of the house facing the water, where my grandmother and Uncle Jim and Auntie Leta, all in white, sipped tea in the steamer chairs. Bracey runs back and forth on the pristine boards, barking happily.

Tying up loose ends is not Gary's style. Having concluded

what he sees as his part of the job, he moves on, while Jorge, another master carpenter, finishes the details. Jorge is a perfectionist, an archangel, a miracle-maker with a John-the-Baptist beard and a gentle, Spanish-accented voice. If I mention a leak of cold air in the bedroom floor over the porch, he goes at the matter with the tenaciousness of a dachshund after a mole. I make lists of these cracks, slits in my citadel, as fifty-mile-an-hour winds send chilly arrows across my ankles and shoulders, and Jorge vanquishes them, one by one. He tracks down small and large leaks, subtle whiffs and prolonged breezes, putting his cheeks to the floorboards, Bracey behind him, sniffing in his wake. He uses cans of foam, silicone tubes, caulking guns, climbing on ladders to apply glues—puffy, spreading gels, gums, and clear liquids—to the cracks and holes above windows, around doors, behind shelves.

Bracey is in ecstasy poking his nose in the cans and tubes, which I keep moving out of his reach. He worships Jorge, this bearded fellow with his tools, this Old Testament visionary. Head on paws, totally absorbed, his eyes follow Jorge's quiet, meticulous hands as they lift the treasures—the planes and saws and bits—from his fabulous chest of instruments. These, by his gifted labor, Jorge makes sing.

Bracey listens, rapt, making a connection, perhaps, with the other sorts of music he loves. When I tie my shoes in the front hall, he bursts forth in a full bass baritone as a prelude to our walk. He sounds much like Tito Gobbi or Bryn Terfel. Just yesterday, his bottom register had a beautiful sheen, like a clarinet.

He's what Uncle Jim dreamed of being, an Opera Tenor! "Didn't I ever tell you my three secret wishes?" Uncle Jim writes in a letter to a student. "(1) To write *one* good sonnet. (2) To talk, *one hour*, French with a perfect style and accent. (3) To be an Opera Tenor, right in the limelight, *for one evening only*. I couldn't stand more than one of each."

Bravissimo, Uncle Jim!

Addition on the outside, facing the vegetable garden

Each time there's a waltz on the radio, Bracey comes to me and—I know this may sound silly—asks me to dance, the way we did in New York. Floating together over the polished floor, we gaze out the new windows at sea and spruce, islands and hills, both of us smiling.

In early summer, as Bracey and I sit on the open, south porch, I say to him, "Some people travel to Europe for edification, but you know? I really am happy staying right here." I massage his long nose. "Steinbeck started his *Travels with Charley* at this house, with Charley by his side, just as you are now, Bracey sweetheart, by mine—you who have so valiantly and faithfully aided me in my long search for a home. We don't need to go anywhere."

The addition is finished. Jorge departed two weeks ago, taking his enchanted toolbox along with him. I eat lunch at the round table with crooked legs. Bracey keeps his eye on a raft of eiders drifting along the shore. His white paws fidget slightly.

"Now I'm ready to screen in this porch—the one on the north

is too small and dark and has no view," I say, puffed up like a real estate mogul, like Donald Trump. I swat a mosquito buzzing at my cheek.

I peer sideways into the adjacent, bedimmed living room where my family ghosts sit, as usual, by the fire. Uncle Jim reads Amy Lowell. Auntie Leta knits a pair of cinnamon-colored socks. Great-grandmother Letitia dreams mistily of Ireland. Aware of them every time I voyage through the living room to this porch, I'm silent in their presence. The quieter I am, the less they will notice me, I think: a mouse down her hole, a mole in her tunnel.

I've become more audacious, however. I built onto their house, after all. Is it overbold to consider adding screens to this porch, as well?

"Perhaps it's more culturally enriching to stroll down Vézelay's grand aisle or through Palladio's villas in Vicenza," I say to Bracey, biting into my cheddar cheese sandwich. "I prefer my porch. But screens *would* help."

Bracey hunts for scraps of food—always hopeful I'll drop crumbs or pieces of cheese—among the crooked legs.

"From the porch, Penobscot Bay looks as good as the Bay of Naples or the Aegean Sea," I say to Bracey. "Too good for the likes of us, huh?"

I dip into Uncle Jim's *Letters and Writings*, which I brought out with me to the porch. In a letter from Sorrento to my mother when she was a teenager, he says: "How can I write about all we see. It is entrancing, heavenly! Everything is funny. Naples was funnier than a flock of goats. Capri was beyond its reputation. The sunny morning yesterday gave us a glimpse of heaven and the sea took on the blue which belongs to it."

Well, yes, but we have our own heaven right here. "I'm done traveling," I say, wiping cheese from my mouth. "I don't need to go anyplace."

White-winged scoters scoot low over the waves. They pause to dillydally along Dunham's Ledge.

I consider offering Bracey a wedge of cheddar.

"I can't afford to go to Europe anymore, anyway, truth be told. Not with this house on my hands."

Mist feathers over Eagle Island's lighthouse, plumes of fog fasten on Bradbury's steep, dense profile, and translucent clouds slip down the mulberry sides of the Camden Hills.

Resolved, by now, on screening in the porch, I call Wayne, my new contractor, from the porch using my cordless phone. Hard Head bulks in the bay, whale-like.

"Will you make the south porch into a screened porch?" I ask. This construction business has gone to my head!

"If that's what you want," Wayne says.

In the living room, I observe Uncle Jim slowly close his book. Tall and elegant, he rises and straightens his buff-yellow bow tie.

"You're too fat, Bracey, baby," I say. "You look like one of those *putti* on San Lorenzo."

Auntie Leta taps the tips of her needles together, a staccato sound, rolls the cinnamon socks up, and places them in her crocheted knitting bag.

Bracey wags his tail-less rump.

Great-grandmother Letitia adjusts her shawl.

Is another screened porch the icing on the cake, or simply *de trop*, as Georgette would have said? I become irresolute.

But a week later, Wayne starts on my Parthenon on a Porch: he constructs five narrow columns on the long south side, and two each on the shorter sides, which also have screen doors. The openings between each column are about five feet wide by ten feet high.

Bracey is once again enraptured. Life without builders has been colorless, dull.

Wayne, who has close-cropped brown hair and a prosthetic arm, makes screens to fit and neatly inserts them—like the bas-reliefs on the Erechtheum—between the columns one by one: the larger, seven-foot screens on top, the smaller, one-and-a-half-foot screens on the bottom. I am amazed at the precision of his work.

Screened porch—see-through temple and art gallery

"They fit perfectly," I marvel.

Wayne, clearly pleased, holds them up to the view, as though showing paintings at Sotheby's. How much would I give for these? I wonder, as he places each screen into its opening. I stand helplessly, nervously, in love with the process, this transformation of the open porch into see-through temple into art gallery.

That panel with the section of Butter Island—with the curved beach and the red meadow—is particularly choice, I think to myself. Pure Fitz Hugh Lane, the air crystalline, the horizon tinged with pink.

Wayne holds up a smaller screen in which common eiders gather around the rocks off my shore. I like that, too. Martin Johnson Heade, in his favorite small, horizontal format, every detail surrealistically distinct.

Did I need a screened porch, a filter, to permit me to look at my view? Do I need my ghosts' consent?

My Uffizi

I walk around the three walls of seascapes and landscapes, noting the conditions of weather and ordered effects of chiaroscuro, the use of stilled time, the muted, tonal harmony of colors, the pervading luminosity.

I'm like a crazed billionaire admiring the vast collection of paintings in his penthouse.

"You could see out better before I made these screens," Wayne says.

Bracey looks up sharply.

"But your work enhances the view," I say. He's made the porch into a collection of Marsden Hartleys, Winslow Homers, and John Marins. Botticellis and Canalettos. Mughal paintings from Kashmir, even. He's made it into my own little Uffizi, Prado, Louvre, Metropolitan.

Wayne laughs and shakes his head. He offers Bracey a Twinkie.

In a few days, a large family from Long Island with six grandchildren will take over the house. Bracey and I will have to remove ourselves to the Trivet, where we will dwell in obsequiousness.

I may dream of the Prado and Uffizi, of the Metropolitan and Pratap Singh Museum in Srinagar, but I have a house to support.

⤜ 11 ⤛

TELLTALES

After spending the summer in the Trivet, Bracey and I have returned to the big house. It's early December now. The cook-stove-cum-heater, beside which I do my writing, provides welcome warmth in the kitchen, but if I'm to stay here another winter, I'll need a proper furnace, I realize. It will have to be small, of course, to fit in the downstairs bathroom, the only space for it. A bold thought, putting in a furnace. I'm still amazed at these flights of explosive practicality. Pearl Hardie, one of my nearest neighbors, who lives a mile and a half down the road, plows us out during snowstorms, though he does us last, since I don't have a job to get to. Sometimes I'm marooned for twenty-four hours, no way to exit, with drifts of snow as high as five feet blocking the driveway. Exciting and exhilarating and achingly beautiful. Two days ago, Pearl arrived in his truck with the plow, lights flashing.

"How ya doin', Brenda?" he shouted out his window, flecks of snow blowing onto his eyebrows.

"Fine, fine," I cried, while Bracey tunneled into the piles of snow thrown up by the plow.

"Let's take a walk to Sylvester's Cove today," I say to my boy this morning. At the mere sound of the word walk, Bracey scrambles from his bed by the stove and heads for the door. Out the window, snowflakes flutter to the plowed driveway, settling on the gravel like tiny, crystal starfish. Another storm.

"Hey, wait a minute," I say, munching on Cheerios. "Will you allow me to finish my breakfast, please?" He patters back to the kitchen, plants himself purposefully next to my chair, and scrutinizes each spoonful of cereal as I raise it to my mouth.

In the hall, I put on my blue-and-white parka. "We'll make it to the cove and back before the storm hits really hard," I say.

The cove, totally empty now of the sailboats and lobster boats of summer, is about a mile from the house. On our way, we pass birch trees leaning into the frozen black swamp, branches caught in the ice, bent twigs embedded in Miró-shaped swirls. Bracey sniffs for signs of life among the congealed roots, ever hopeful.

I look through the windows of three summerhouses clustered where the road curves down toward the water. Sea urchins, sand dollars, and mussel shells adorn windowsills, mixed with jacks and tiny rubber figures of dragons and pirates. Copies of Alice Duer Miller's popular 1940s novels and books of poetry anchor sheets that have been draped over tables and chairs. Kids' slickers and binoculars hang on wooden hooks by the front doors.

Observing these items, I think of my own, blooming expectations of summer days—of sailing alone and singing to the clouds and gulls; of yearning for a companion with whom to share this ecstasy, even as I rejoiced in my solitude; later, of romancing on the water, of being romanced. Sloughing off my mousy brown, schoolgirl guise, I learned to don snazzy halter-tops and shorts, to be a show-off sailor. It was sexy to sail well, to know the wind and currents, to laugh out in the middle of the bay, heeled over in a brisk northwest wind.

Out on the water, singing to the clouds and gulls

I invited occasional beaux to Deer Isle, ones I felt could withstand the pronginess of the Braces, and took them sailing. If they weren't already sailors, I demonstrated how: I held their hands gently on the tiller, guided their eyes to the luff in the sail, the telltales on the stays. And if they were, I was indisputably their equal.

For one beau in particular, I pulled out all my sailing tricks: took him around Eagle—under the lighthouse, close to the bell buoy—and told him sailing yarns. I decided I'd marry him. Wickedly charming, he was perfect.

Back in New York, however, I gave him away, sent him with a note of introduction to take to a friend of mine in Paris, where he went visiting.

A cable came, and flowers.

"We're engaged. Thank you!"

"Why, for God's sake, did you do that?" friends asked. "Why did you give him *away*?"

"Did I?" I asked. "I didn't realize."

But, of course, this is just what I'd done. Other men I gave away by drinking, by leaving messes—causing disagreements and fights.

Snow blurs our journey. As we move along, Bracey digs his nose under the whiteness, stopping, from time to time, to bite at it, to lap it up with gusto.

I started out my working life in New York City in my parents' apartment at Ninety-sixth and Park. Living in Brussels, where my father was U.S. minister with the Marshall Plan, my parents kept their New York apartment for a couple of years. I shared the place with four roommates, who paid a nominal rent. Which meant I got off free. We threw cocktail parties that often went on all night. One time, I discovered a particularly helpful guest vacuuming at 7 a.m.

After my parents gave up their apartment, I found my own places. Almost every two years, I changed my address. We all did this. Someone would tell you at a party that he was moving out of his fantastic, inexpensive digs on East Ninetieth, for example, and you'd grab it. Musical apartments. Either I shared with roommates or lived alone in cheap, one-room, fifth-floor walkups.

I took the Lexington Avenue subway to work every day. The Lex was clubby. You'd meet friends, hang close together from adjacent straps, energized, the day offering unknown excitements, work still a new experience, with unaccustomed responsibilities. For a while, I was part of this fabled work force, a keen, young face in the swaying multitude, with common destinations, all equal in a sense, lots of dates, dancing after work in nightclubs, gallons of drink.

One morning, I woke up somewhere. In bed with someone. Who? I looked at his face.

My halter-top dress

Chap I liked the night before at Judy's party on the Upper West Side. Real glamour boy. Princeton. Job on Wall Street. Waspy. Wealthy. Not the kind I usually ended up with: Harvard nerd, professor's son, historian's nephew.

How had I landed him? Drink. Five martinis on West Eight-ninth Street, three Scotches in bar in Greenwich Village, untold stingers here, in this townhouse.

I got out of bed and walked downstairs to the living room. Bodies everywhere: draped on the damask sofa, stretched on the Turkoman rug. Girl with red hair looped over curly blond lad.

No one was awake.

Back up to my beautiful guy—brown hair mussed, cheek on lacy pillowcase, suit on floor.

I looked for my pink pumps—under the bed, in the bathroom. Slipped into my rayon sheath. Down the stairs again, out onto the street.

"Where am I?" I asked a passerby.

The road just now is covered in snow. Bracey's and my footprints mark our path behind us, except for the occasional, exploratory paw prints to the side of the road.

My first real job was at Durlacher Bros. Art Gallery on Fifty-seventh Street, where I was the assistant-cum-secretary. I typed letters, paid bills, made appointments, and did research on paintings on consignment. My big moments were when the dealers, Mr. Askew, gray-haired and husky-voiced, and Mr. Dix, blond and kindly, left for their long, three-martini lunches with collectors and dealers and I was alone in the gallery. Once, a short man with a suitcase that seemed to smell of fish came in. We had a show of twelve Francis Bacons at the time.

"I'll take six of them," he said, after looking at the paintings in the front gallery for around fifteen minutes. "That one, that one, and that one . . . At thirty percent off."

"But we don't give discounts," I said, shaking in my pumps. Mr. Askew and Mr. Dix had commanded me over and over: "Do not ever give discounts to *anyone*. Ever."

The man picked up his rather odiferous suitcase. "Do you mean that?" he scowled at me. "Did your bosses tell you to say that?"

"Yes."

At which, he strode out the gallery without a word, handing me his card before banging the door behind him. I looked at it and collapsed on the round red ottoman in the center of the room: Joseph H. Hirshhorn. Surely I would lose my job. I was finished. The art world was abuzz with news about his buying. He was from Canada and planning a large museum in the U.S.

When Mr. Askew and Mr. Dix came back from lunch, I gave them the card, rigid with fright.

"You did the right thing," they both said. "Absolutely the right thing."

"I felt relieved, but didn't believe them, of course," I say to Bracey, stopping to squeeze a handful of snow into a snowball and throw it to him. "I didn't have the confidence." He snaps at it, and it falls apart in his mouth. Vanishes. Poof. He looks all over for it on the road. "But I might now." I smile into the soft grains falling from the low, pasty sky.

I have another memory from about that same time. I was back in New York after visiting my parents in Brussels.

"Are you American?" he said. "You don't *look* American. What are you? Speak and I'll know."

We were standing by the drinks table in the small kitchen of an apartment on East Seventy-second Street. About fifteen people were crowded around it; another thirty stood in the living room beyond. We surveyed the bottles of Scotch, bourbon, vodka, rum, white and red vermouth, Cinzano, brandy; the tonic water and club soda; the jugs of water and white wine and cans of tomato juice; the strips of lemon, wedges of lime, and cocktail onions; the plastic glasses, cocktail napkins, and silver ice bucket. I was positively damp from sprays of vodka and soda as guests swung the bottles around, pouring everyone cocktails: Manhattans, screwdrivers, martinis with a twist of lemon, vodka Gibsons, Rob Roys, whiskey sours, old fashioneds, Scotches and soda, bourbons on the rocks with a dash of Worcestershire sauce, spiked eggnog.

He wasn't American, that much was clear. A Cockney? He looked like Cary Grant. Grinning at me, he had large, mischievous brown eyes, good teeth.

It was 2 p.m. on New Year's Day, 1954. My third year out of college. The night before, at a party down in the Village, I'd thrown my wine glass into a fireplace in celebration of the new year; other guests had done the same—I wasn't totally out of control or anything. Hung over the next morning, I hadn't wanted to come to this party.

I eyed a bottle of Gilbey's gin.

"Can I make you a drink?" he asked.

I inhaled the perfume of alcohol that rose from the table. I wasn't rolling yet. I needed time, fuel. This guy was fresh, pushy, you could say—but I sort of liked it.

"Gin martini straight up," I said, "light on the vermouth, with an olive."

It was a job, making drinks among all the hands and arms criss-crossing the table, a frenzy of writhing serpents. But the martini he handed me was perfect.

"You're American," he shouted.

"Well, technically, I'm a British subject," I said. "But, I'm an American, too. I've just been in Brussels, seeing my parents. What are *you?*"

"Australian. Although, I hate Australia. Too conservative."

We edged our way into the living room. Blaikie, one of the hostesses and a classmate from Milton, as well as an ex-roommate from Ninety-sixth Street, came over.

"You've met Mitchell! He's a friend of Harriet's cousin Pete. They're both at the Harvard Business School."

Christ, I'd never wanted to know anyone from the Harvard Business School.

"Is Mitchell your first name?"

"No, it's Bill."

"But you're called Mitchell?"

"Yeah. Dunno why," he said. "What do you do?"

"I work at an art gallery on Fifty-seventh Street. You?"

"I'm an engineer, polishing up my business skills."

Jesus.

"The fact is, I'm European," I said, not knowing what else to say to a budding engineer/businessman. "I belong over there. I *have* no home."

"Well, you look downright healthy to me."

We sat on a low beige sofa by the window facing Seventy-second Street. Mitchell had to crunch up his long legs. I could see the building where my grandmother and Eleanor and Muriel had lived, before my grandmother died and Eleanor and Muriel moved up to Wiscasset. A grand old pre-war with an awning, it looked much the same as it had when I was a child.

"You've met Mitchell!" said my other hostess/Milton classmate/ ex-roommate, Harriet, as she passed by with a tray of smoked salmon on pumpernickel rounds. "He's a friend of Pete's. Has he told you yet he's at the Harvard Business School?"

Was this a set up?

"The Royale on the Grand' Place in Brussels makes the best *moules marinières* I ever ate," he said, ignoring Harriet. He observed me slyly out of the corner of his eye.

His French accent was atrocious.

"I had my portrait painted by an artist who lives on the Grand' Place," I said. I primped my permed, dark brown hair.

"Magritte, *par chance?*" he said. "The chap with the pipe and all that?" He was irresistibly de trop. A crazy, improbable guess. But, hey, not entirely ignorant of art.

"Oh, sure, and exploding tubas to you, too," I retorted.

Our martini glasses were at this point empty. I watched him cross the living room and disappear into the smoke, his brown head towering above the other guests. He returned after a few moments, holding the glasses together in his hands while using his elbows to open his way back. A gangly, handsome ranchero all of a sudden, he was on his farm in Queensland, loping through a thousand Merinos.

"Do you have sheep?" I asked, as he sat down.

"No, I lived in a city, Adelaide," he said. "I have an idea. Let me take you around Central Park in a horse and carriage, will you?"

A rube. I'd never been in one of those touristy hacks. Neither—like most native New Yorkers—had I been up the Empire State Building.

"I have to work tomorrow," I said. "Have to think about Hyman Bloom and Alessandro Masaccio."

"Never heard of 'em," he joked, though he was also telling the truth, and lifted his martini to his lips.

"At least, you've heard of Magritte!" I said. "Oh, well, you poor thing, I'll plainly have to teach you."

"But first, let's go to the Ambassador to dance," he said.

Two weeks later, in my tight-fitting, royal blue silk-rayon sheath with matching shoes from Saks, I was in his arms, fox-trotting to "Speak Low" at the Ambassador Hotel. He was a good dancer, no question, had a firm hand at my back.

"Marry me," he said, and drew me to him cheek-to-cheek. The tuxedoed band players and ringside patrons passed by in luminescent loops, flashing and blazing as we danced round and round. I was airborne.

"Too soon!"

Bracey and I pass the field where a single apple tree, supported by a wooden crutch, tilts precariously. Flakes stream into my face. Bracey lowers his head and squints his eyes, no longer tempted to make side trips into the deepening snow beside the road.

"Haven't seen you much in daylight," Mitchell said on the phone one May morning from his office in Midtown. He had started work at GE. I was at my small desk inside the painting stacks at Durlacher's. A naked bulb hung from the ceiling. At the far end of the tunnel, in a back room bathed in north light, my bosses were displaying a George Stubbs painting of a horse to clients, who sat on the brown, plush velvet sofa with soft cushions. "The quality of the brushstroke here, in this corner, is texturally delectable," said one of the clients, a curator from the National Gallery of Art, I believe. He bent toward the painting, magnifying glass to his eye. From my desk, I could smell the smoke from Mr. Askew's Lucky Strike.

"That's because I hate daylight," I said.

"Let's go for a walk in Central Park on Saturday. Then you can show me the paintings at the Met."

Here I am—expat-cum-student—in my parents' Paris apartment

As Mitchell and I strolled toward the Seventy-second Street boat pond, daffodils bobbed on the rises and hillocks along the path. In the middle of the pond, a tiny red sloop had tipped over, its sail flopped on the surface of the water like a carelessly folded linen napkin on a glass tabletop. The wind pushed the boat sideways toward the concrete edge where, I observed, a little girl in a navy blue school blazer and her nanny sat waiting.

The girl, thin and tentative, knelt on the rim and reached out toward the sloop, which was drifting beyond her, several times with a boat hook. Finally, she stood up and looked at her nurse. Would she give in and ask her nurse to take over, I wondered? Is that what I would have done in her place? No, she knelt back down again, this time catching the boat and pulling it to safety. The nanny led the girl, who silently carried the dripping sailboat in her arms, up the hill toward Fifth Avenue.

"I had a nanny," I said, as we watched her. "I didn't talk as a child, either. I was timid. I still don't talk much."

"You're a good waltzer, though," Mitchell said, caressing my hand, "and damned stubborn."

At the Met, we mounted the grand staircase. In a European paintings gallery, howling winds hurled at the foundering ship, hove to on her beam end, and ripped the topgallant, mizzen, and mainsail to shreds. Sails blew out from gaskets and reefs. Lashed to the rigging, mates and seamen skidded down the perpendicular decks, dragged by torrents of water; hands gripped rails and stays in the long slide, fingers disappeared over the sides into the roiling sea.

Mitchell put his arm around my shoulders and held me tight as we looked at this wonderful early Turner.

"He was big on the Sublime, and on cosmic catastrophes," I said.

Mitchell was silent, looking at the picture respectfully. "We'll travel the world by sea, air, rail," Mitchell said, at last. He stroked my arm.

Terror rose in me all at once. *I* was on that ship foundering at sea. I held onto the weather rail as the boards slanted under me, my legs dangling in the solid stream. Pigs and chickens hurtled past me down the sloping deck, eyes red, shrieking and cackling with fear.

"You've done it before," he said. "So you know the ropes."

I thought of my father now, how similar he and Mitchell were to one another: affable, cheerful, adaptable, detached. Both were tall and slim, too, though Mitchell carried himself with a bit of an outback swagger, a touch of bush defensiveness.

My father had danced with me. He'd patted me, stroked me, my mother watching. Her black eyes spoke to me, to her approval of this affection. Did he know what he was doing? I doubt it now—almost. After all, it was at my mother's bidding. Of course, he also had a tender, highly physical generosity.

The storm inside had only worsened. I slipped on the wet, vertical planks. The mast broke and fell overboard. A pretty hen with a feathery brown and white crown whirled in the spoondrift. The air was full of salt water. I could hardly breathe.

Mitchell smiled at me, steadied me with his arm.

"Right now, though, let's have a drink," he said.

We kissed in the taxi ride down Fifth Avenue to the St. Regis, past rows of apartment buildings on the east and blooming cherry trees on the west.

Mitchell was a spender. We drank in hotel bars, ate in French restaurants, always had good theater seats.

Maxfield Parrish's King Cole over the bar was jolly. I relaxed.

"You look smashing, ducks," Mitchell toasted. "Here's to mates."

The snow, driven by the northeast wind, spirals and twists by the time Bracey and I arrive at Sylvester's Cove. Barely visible, the beach is iced over and the spruces dusted a heavy white. Bracey trudges manfully by my side.

This is more of a storm than I'd expected—a big one for early December. I'm a lone adventurer, marching in reindeer boots with my dog across the glazed rubble of the North Pole, like Fridtjof Nansen, the Arctic explorer. Nansen had once wooed my mother, as it happens, in Geneva, when he and my father were both with the League of Nations. He'd wanted her to leave her husband and two sons (I wasn't born yet) and run away with him.

Snow increases on the road. The wind could knock me down. Were I to fall and break my ankle, I could freeze like the birch logs in the swamp, join them in the deep, black ice. No one travels this way in winter.

"Come down to Caracas. See where I live," Mitchell summoned over the phone from Venezuela. GE had sent him there in 1959, soon after I'd returned to New York from helping organize the art shows in the U.S. Pavilion at the Brussels World's Fair. I almost hadn't taken the Brussels job in order to stay in New York to be with Mitchell, but we talked it over. "It won't be for long," I pleaded. Mitchell agreed, although reluctantly. It was a big step up in my career, not to mention a chance to go back to Brussels under my own steam.

In Brussels, I played around, saw some of my old Dutch beaux. The summer after my Smith College Junior Year in Paris, I'd met a group of good-looking law students in Amsterdam through Blaikie and became entangled with several of them, almost to the point of marrying one. This time I also got a little involved with a Polish count. Oh, and there was an American in Paris . . .

"This is my ultimatum," Mitchell said. (We were in our sixth year.) What could I say?

Jungle heat hit me at the Caracas airport. Whereupon, we drove three thousand feet up steep mountain passes to the city, its tall, white buildings at the head of a valley surrounded by peaks. Thousands of huts spilled over the mountainsides. Lush purple and dusty pink flowers cascaded over garden walls.

I felt trapped on this high, elliptical plateau: the only way back was down the looping mountain road to the tropical coast—a week from now, the date on my return ticket.

Mitchell wanted to live all over the world, wanted me by his side—much the way my mother was by my father's, I thought—an international bride. The prospect was both thrilling and familiar, a continuation of my earlier life: expatriate, intense, teasingly strange; always new places and friends, never any roots, any real sense of home. I could live again in different cities abroad, as I always had with my family: in London (before we moved out to Roehampton)—in a small townhouse in a cul-de-sac; in Paris—in a vast apartment with balconies above the trees and boulevards; in Karachi—in marble rooms with ceiling fans and printed textiles and mirrored, tasseled cushions.

We'd start in Caracas, in his modern apartment with a balcony overlooking the mountains and shantytowns and a mango tree that blossomed in the yard below. Next, we might move on, to a house in Rangoon, perhaps, and an apartment in Singapore. I'd always be a foreigner, but I'd be special.

"I'm off to work now," he said the next morning. "You'll be all right? Why don't you go out? To a museum or something."

I sat on the balcony, on the bed. I didn't go anywhere. I knew I should marry him. I was overwhelmed.

"What did you do today?" he asked when he returned. I didn't know what to say.

We ate in garden restaurants on mountain ridges. Bands played Venezuelan waltzes. Scented salmon and white orchids projected over our tables, tumbled everywhere; frilled lemon-yellow hibiscus, translucent in the long twilight, grew in rondels on sloping lawns. I'd never seen so much flowering; the sweet air pressed behind my eyes.

Mitchell instructed me how to take the bus to the central Plaza Simón Bolívar. The next morning I walked among its fountains, statues, and formal beds of red and purple bougainvillea.

Mitchell and me

I took another bus to Villanueva's modern University City. Colossal, exposed-concrete buildings bulked on the campus. The austerity frightened me. I could disappear in this eerie space, I thought, macerated by the cantilevered, sharp-ribbed Olympic Stadium, swallowed by the fistulous, gray Faculty Building. Eventually, I found my way back to Mitchell's apartment—from one fearsome situation to another.

"Did you go inside the Auditorium?" Mitchell asked that evening. "Did you see the Calders floating under the ceiling?"

"So you know your Calders," I smiled feebly.

In Europe, I'd been a *cicerone*. I'd taken friends on motor trips to Burgundy, Italy, Norway. Visiting my parents and later when I was with the Fair in Brussels, I drove miles to see buildings in Ghent and Bruges, Paris and Laon, Amsterdam and The Hague.

I didn't tell him how panicked the Auditorium's concrete shells had left me, those windswept terraces facing the metal-roofed huts.

"There's a Calder mobile hanging over the stairs at the museum, actually," I said. I'd taken a job at the Museum of Modern Art after my return to New York from Brussels. "I see it every day I come to work."

Damn. Too smart-ass. We can't afford this sort of rhythm anymore.

"You don't see buildings by Villanueva every day," he said, a little fretfully.

Too right.

"Why did you come?" he asked our last night. We were dancing outdoors on a smooth round platform. A macaw jumped up and down on his swing, quavering zarzuela love songs.

We belonged together. I'd felt this since I first met him. My mother was crazy about him. My friends found him amusing. My brothers thought I should marry him. My aunt on Cape Cod wrote I'd always regret it if I didn't marry him. On his own, he'd visited Eleanor in Maine. Startled when he arrived on her doorstep without me, she was in the end taken, indeed, charmed by him. We were meant to marry, I knew that. Which is why I didn't believe I could.

The next day, we descended the endless, steep, curving, shadowed mountain road to the airport by the sea. Hotels built on the Caracas littoral by Peréz Jiménez, abandoned after the rebellion against him in 1958, stood among the palm trees, next to empty blue swimming pools. We didn't speak.

Only on the plane did I feel safe. My "life in between."

Mitchell

Bracey and I trudge back through the heavy, wet snow, which now covers the swamp. Birches, their trunks arched under its weight, drink the snow like moose slurping the bottom of a pond. Keeping my head down, I pull my pink knit hat over my eyebrows and ears.

"It's over," Mitchell said in New York, almost a year after my trip to Venezuela. He'd been making frequent trips to the U.S. on business and to see me. "I can't wait any longer."

We sat at the tiny dining table in my studio apartment. His eyes were impatient, sad. I needed more time, I thought. I needed forever.

"Give me another year," I said. "I shall collapse if we part."

Chocolaty brown bourguignon sauce pooled on the plates between us, the remains of my beef stew. He moved his fork in the sauce, making straight lines with the tines, railway tracks, or a highway, out of there.

He'd left once before. "You're difficult," he'd said, "but there's no one else like you."

His mouth was bunched now, his cheeks taut, jaw muscles clenching and then releasing. I thought of the oxen I saw as a child on Dunham's Point hauling spruce logs in a cart, their great sides straining, pulling, lines like wires strung from their necks to their thighs, the hide as tight as a shoe.

He tapped his fingers against the table.

I watched with sad certainty.

Soon he would depart, walk out the door, down the five flights onto Eighty-third Street, step onto a train in the pits of the earth, look out the window at the dark tunnel walls, stare back at his face passing before an oblivion of slick, gray rock.

"Are you ill?" asked a friend, having phoned for the fourth time. I hadn't come to work at the museum for a couple of days.

The sun set over the parapet of the brownstone tenement across the street. From my rose sofa bed, I watched two girls, who'd been sunbathing on the tar roof—one in a turquoise tank suit, the other in a two-piece zebra pattern—carry their deck chairs to the stairwell. Wedged around me were piles of the *New York Times*, *New Yorker*, *Time Magazine*, and *Art News*. Listening to Handel and Haydn on WQXR, I'd been going to pieces. I couldn't venture outdoors in this condition. I tried once and made it back to the apartment just in time.

"I'm fine, really, I'm fine," I said. "I'll call you tomorrow."

A red ceramic mug with instant Maxwell House coffee sat on

Snow squall

a table drawn up to my sofa bed, right next to a jelly jar glass of vodka and a prescription bottle of valium. I held the hot mug against my cheek, shifted it to my nose, then my forehead and eyes. The heat drew out the tears, flushed them from the deep river that pitched inside my ribs, sloshed against the sides of my stomach.

There's a snow squall by the time Bracey and I climb the last hill to my mailbox. Bracey plods beside me, his deep chest plowing the drifts, ears flattened, nose barely above snow level. From here to the house is easy. It's right at the end of the driveway. But we can't see it, the snow altogether blinding. We're almost upon it, when the house looms suddenly like the hull of a great ship.

FOR THE MOMENT

"The sills are rotten," Wayne says with grim satisfaction in the spring, the season of renovation. "The foundation posts are crumbling." He sounds like a doctor diagnosing a hip fracture.

We stand among the rosa rugosas behind the Trivet, examining the small cabin for repairs. Our heads are level with the tops of the old, mullioned windows. I hadn't seen Wayne very much over the winter. There'd been no emergencies or indoor construction work or downed trees. Bracey and I have only just moved to the Trivet from the big house, which has been rented for the whole season. Bracey, who gnaws on a spruce twig, listens to our conversation with intense curiosity. Anything Wayne does is always of interest.

Wayne points his crowbar at a band of gray, moldy mush low down on the wall, hardly recognizable as wood. Bracey drops his twig and trots over to sniff at the spongy pulp.

"How much will it cost to fix the sills and foundation?" I ask with dread. I've gone overboard with construction projects the last year, spent all my money. I panic.

"Don't know," Wayne says. "Depends on what else I find when I go in there. Maybe a week's worth, maybe more . . ."

Where am I going to get the cash for this? All the money from the big house rentals goes back into the house. The little I earn from editing museum catalogs for the Princeton Art Museum certainly won't cover this job.

"How will I pay for this?" I say.

"Rent out this one, too!" Wayne says cheerfully.

"But I'll be without a house, a home—exiled!" I protest. "I've only been back in the Trivet a few days!"

The Trivet's built-in dining alcove

He starts to rip the festering timber with the crowbar.

"Wait! Wait!" I say. "Let me see if I can rent the Trivet first!"

Bracey, having detected the alarm in my voice, stops sniffing a deliciously sodden pile of blackened leaves and turns in my direction.

I put an ad in the local paper: "Picturesque period piece. 1920s charm. Chintz curtains, built-in dining alcove with benches, fireplace, wicker chairs, screen porch. Available end July/August." That'll give Wayne and me time to get the Trivet in shape.

"Oh, yes, there's a spectacular view of the bay," I say a few days later on the phone to a couple in Vermont who have responded to the ad.

Perched on one of the window seats by the fireplace, I see caliginous clouds, layered over ribbons of blue sky, gather above the Camden Hills.

"We'll take it the last week in July," they say.

The next day Wayne begins tearing off the Trivet's back sill. He's brought his partner, Charlie—another dog lover, who offers Bracey Oreos—to help. Bracey, happily observing them, soon gets rotund on Twinkies and Oreos.

I, on the other hand, observe it all with relentless fear and anxiety.

My nerves are frayed. Between the renters' six grandchildren screaming their lungs out at the big house and the electric drills and saws whining away at the Trivet, I want to screech myself.

Looking for *something* to do while Wayne and Charlie hammer the new sills in place, I clean the kitchen cabinets and, afterward, wash the china- and glassware. I stuff my belongings out of sight as best I can—in the tops of the minuscule closets, beneath the bed, behind the curtains. I stow them under the benches in the dining alcove and below the windows facing the water.

Run out of both the big house and the Trivet, the question now is: Where do Bracey and I go?

I call Nancy, who writes violent, dark stories. She's going to the Stonecoast Writers Conference in a week. "Can I come along?" I ask. "Is it too late to sign up? Can Bracey stay with Dan while we're gone?" Dan is Nancy's husband, a painter of sublime watercolors.

"Yes, no, yes," she answers.

"Oh, that's super!" I say. "I have to be out of here in a week."

"Well, good!" she says.

The vegetable garden is in full view of the big house. Now that it's almost the end of July, every time I notice that the tenants have left to go sightseeing, I rush over to prepare, in bursts of frenzied activity, sections of the garden for the late summer and fall. I pull out rows of wilted, yellowed lettuce and greens. I turn the soil with a tall, wooden-handled digging fork and mix in composted cow manure. I sow Lollo Rossa and Hyper Red Rumple Waved lettuce for an August/September crop; Andover parsnips and Nantes Fancy carrots for October. Brussels sprouts, well under way, will produce until the snows come.

The vegetable garden

While the tenants sleep one morning, I pick a salad of early Sun Gold tomatoes and oak leaf lettuce, which I take back to the Trivet and eat for my lunch on its small screen porch. I toss a few of the small tomatoes to Bracey, who delights in catching them. Our ritual reminds me of my social life in the 1950s, when I nonchalantly tossed boyfriends about. It's all there in an Airletter I sent to my old friend Blaikie, in Paris at the time, on August 12, 1952, and which she recently returned to me. Just turned twenty-three, I was in New York: "Thanks for your postcard," I wrote. "I could barely manage to pick it up from the floor, where it had fallen, what with marketbag in arms and general dissipation. . . . Nothing much has happened. Weekend ago went sailing in New Haven with Fred. Last night Dick and his roommates came over—nice, but not terrifically impressive. Tonight go to 'Pal Joey' with Bill, recent conquest. Am still working on Kenneth, with no success. . . . I'm sure there must be something vital to say. . . . Have fun and bring me back a Dior evening dress!"

Tossing men, just like the Sun Golds. That's what I was doing.

The renters in the big house will feast on my Brandywines and

Early Girls, as well as the Sun Golds, while we're gone. Perhaps they'll share the bounty with the Trivet tenants.

"Tomorrow we hit the road," I say to Bracey, as he leaps to catch a tiny tomato. "The Trivet renters are coming. We're *déraciné* again." In the distance, a yawl under Bradbury Island beats north through taupe seas to Eggemoggin Reach.

The next morning, squashing among cartons of books and totes filled with clothing, Bracey and I funnel into my second-hand Subaru Loyale, which I've bought to replace the Chevy. A Rubbermaid cooler rests on the floor in front of the passenger seat. I put Bracey's Bean bed, flannel sheet, dog food, snacks, water bottle, and toys next to him on the back seat, where he now prefers to sit, for some reason, away from the windows. The last time he was in the car, he whined and cried in the front seat until I moved him to the back.

We drive to Nancy and Dan's neat, exquisitely cared-for old cape with an attached barn on Dow Road, four miles away, where I unload Bracey's paraphernalia and take it into the house. A neighbor's dog, Cody, part husky, part German shepherd, sits by the front door. He's beigy white, with brown markings. "A very smart dog," Nancy says. Neglected by his own family, he's at Dan and Nancy's most of the time, waiting for Dan to get into his Taurus wagon so he can race alongside it to the village. Not a car chaser, exactly, he simply likes to demonstrate to Dan his competitive spirit. He's learned to find his kicks where he can, it seems, to be self-reliant and optimistic, his bowl always half full.

Shielded from life's vicissitudes, Bracey's not nearly so inventive, so sanguine. Assertive, a loudmouth even when things are going his way, he shrinks into corners, squeezes under the bathtub at the sound of fireworks or lightning, and sleeps downstairs in high winds or rainfall.

Bracey settles himself beside Cody on the front steps. Companionable in Dan and Nancy's front yard, Bracey and Cody will watch the cars and occasional joggers pass by, content in their proximity to one another, in the security of their surroundings.

At the writers' workshop—my first—in Freeport, we do writing exercises. "Scribble anything you like in five minutes," says the leader of one class. "Five minutes! Anything you like!" Pens tear across pages, noses bend to notebooks, feet tap.

"In five minutes, I can file my nails, wash my hair, eat six Oreos . . ." I begin wildly. Later that day, I fill three wide-ruled notebooks with essays composed in agitated, exhilarated orgies at a wooden table overlooking Casco Bay or, still later, in my dormitory room at 3 a.m. In one essay, I describe raccoons binging on birdseed in my yard. When I read it to the group, the applause is like three martinis straight up.

But I worry about Bracey. Will he be homesick and try to run home? Will he and Cody continue to be friends?

I stew about my tenants in both the big house and the Trivet. Will the beds be comfortable enough? Will the sun shine and the southwest breezes blow?

Mainly what plagues me, however, is my writing. Will I be any good? Will I only produce junk?

How does Cody do it? I wonder. Where does he get that sense of acceptance? Or maybe I should ask Bracey.

When Nancy and I return from the workshop, we find Cody and Bracey by the door, exactly as they were when we left them. Bracey jumps up to greet me with full-throated rapture. His nails make excited skittling noises on the granite steps.

"Were you a good boy?" I say. He rolls on his back, inviting scratches and tickles.

Cody, steady as a rock, doesn't move, though he wags his tail acknowledging us with pleasurable sobriety.

Dan gives us great bear hugs.

"I have a story to tell," he says, his eyes mischievous behind his glasses. "But first, why don't you make yourselves comfortable. Want coffee?"

"Oh, Christ, Dan," I say. "What awful thing did Bracey *do?*" I slump in a deep armchair in the living room, Bracey in my lap. He licks my nose, looking innocent as a newborn babe. Nancy, smiling and hospitable, as always, pokes around in the fridge. Cody remains outside.

"Well, I went off to paint Heart Island, and when I got back Bracey wasn't here! He'd gone. Poof!" Dan says, throwing his arms wide.

I can't stand it. The tension is too much. I look Bracey in the eye, trying to fathom what deviltry he'd been up to.

"Turns out Myrtle, from next door, said she'd seen this strange dog in our yard and had come over and taken him back to the address on the tag on his collar," Dan says.

"'My God, Myrtle,' I said to her. 'Why'dya do that?'" Dan says.

"'I thought he was a runaway,' she said."

He hands me a blue porcelain mug with dark Colombian coffee. Seated on a straight-back chair, his wispy white beard covering his blue denim shirt, he continues: "So I drove over to your house and there he was, having the time of his life with all the renters patting him and giving him Camembert cheese and toasted Wheat Thins."

"Oh dear," I say, "oh dear."

"He was having a ball, my fine little fella." Dan ruffles his chest. "Practically had to drag him back here."

But Cody had been waiting at the door, as always, and apparently Bracey sat right down next to him, ready again to absorb Cody's patient knowingness, to tap into his personal wholeness.

"You're a *brick*, Dan."

"Oh, Bracey's a good, steady kid," he says. "He's my little prince."

Nancy passes around lemon cookies as Dan finishes his story. Bracey placidly licks the long white hair on his paws.

The sun is setting over Butter Island, lighting up the meadow, when Bracey and I come back to the Trivet. An envelope rests on the built-in desk inside. I open it on the screened porch and take out the rent check. I breathe a sigh of relief. For the moment, anyway, the foundation is firm, the sills secure.

More renters are coming to the Trivet the second week in August, however, and so I'll be homeless again. I need a place to go. It's summer, the time for renting, though I've lost track of the years amidst the seasons. Is it 1993 already? Bracey is seven, so it must be.

"Join me at the Marlboro Music Festival," says Beth, a Smith classmate and uncommon pianist, on the phone from Philadelphia when I tell her my situation. "And stay where *I* stay—the Golden Eagle Motel."

"Sounds good," I say.

"'Long as he doesn't get on the bed," says the proprietor of the Golden Eagle Motel over the phone when I ask if one can keep a dog in the room.

"Oh, I never let my corgi sleep on the bed," I lie.

In fact, Bracey *always* sleeps on my bed. I keep a big supply of my aunt's antique, sixty-year-old flannel sheets on hand to protect my blankets from dog hair and dirt. And whenever I travel with Bracey, I take a clean sheet with me. But how is the proprietor going to know if Bracey sleeps on the bed? Is he going to look through my window at night, through the Venetian blind slats or the slit at the bottom of the shade? Still, for a moment I worry that I'm taking advantage of this kind, clearly dog-loving Vermont countryman, that I'm undermining my heart's core with this swift, easy lie.

In a few days, on Saturday, Bracey and I leave at the crack of dawn and make the long drive in my Subaru to the Green Mountains and the motel. Signs along the highway proclaim the area's famous One-Hundred-Mile View. And, true enough, spread over a rise above Route 9, the otherwise undistinguished, rather shabby, two-story motel boasts a stupendous view of mountains receding into an infinitude of green peaks and ridges. Riding up the steep, curved driveway, I park in front of the office, feeling almost as if I'm at base camp on the lower slopes of Mount Everest.

In the mock wood-paneled office, after I press the bell, a woman with light brown hair and cerulean eyes enters. "You have Room 3," she says, and hands me the keys.

"I brought my dog," I offer brightly.

"I know," she says, unsmiling.

I thought she'd wish to see Bracey, admire his rufous good looks and princeliness, and perhaps exclaim over his rare talent for traveling—a breviped mountaineer in the making.

"She didn't even want to meet you," I say to Bracey as I walk back to the car. He sits in the back seat, among his numerous traveling possessions, gazing out the window with intense interest, his dark-rimmed eyes fixed on my every movement.

We drive the few yards to our room and park in front of it. Inside, it's dank and small. Pine-scented Lysol fills the air. Cars block the view of the mountains from the one, tiny window. The double bed fills the room, the boxy TV hangs suffocatingly from the wall, the rug is spotted and faded, and the bathroom has cobwebs in the corners, dirt on the windowsill. Guarded but patient, Bracey sniffs every inch of the place, then waits for me to place his bed and set his dishes out strategically on the grimy floor.

As I begin to unpack, Beth arrives. When I move forward to welcome her, my head bangs against the corner of the TV. Bracey marches over to give her a friendly, inquisitive nuzzle.

"Hello there, Bracey," she says, kneeling down to finger his handsome, red ruff.

"Oh dear, you should see *my* room," she says, looking around. "Come up when you're finished."

I arrange Bracey's things neatly: his suitcase with Hill's Prescription Diet Canine dried chunky dog food, water and food bowls, dog biscuits, and chewies in the bathroom; his Bean bag bed on the stained carpet next to the double bed; his large white flannel sheet on his bed—not on mine, not yet. "We'll see," I say to Bracey. I hang a skirt and two blouses on the three wire hangers.

Bracey and I climb the outer stairs to the second floor to Beth's room, which turns out to have two double beds, an enormous, clean bathroom, and an unobstructed outlook on the area's famous

Marlboro College campus, where the Marlboro Music Festival is held

view. Bracey licks a few drops of water off the shining bathroom floor, and proceeds to roll on the lush, plush, fresh-smelling maroon wall-to-wall. These quarters, he seems to indicate, suit his royal penchants.

"Wow," I say. "This is *splendido*. It's even up to Bracey's standards. Look at him breathing in the mountain breeze wafting through your door. What are you paying for this boudoir?"

"Sixty dollars."

"Sixty dollars! I'm paying almost that amount for my gruesome little hidey-hole!"

On my way back to our room, I stop at the office. Bracey remains serenely postured on the concrete steps, watching the eighteen-wheelers and SUVs out on Route 9. I'm ready to be confrontational, belligerent—up to a point—and then characteristically apologetic, namby-pamby.

In the family room adjacent to the office, the young daughter of the proprietors and a friend stare at elephants swinging their trunks and trumpeting on TV. I see popcorn on the green carpet, cheese doodles scattered on the glass coffee table, an empty Coke can under the TV set, and I think of Bracey's accoutrements, tidily arrayed in our small room, his sparkling, clean sheet spread—innocently—on his bed. My lies about his sleeping arrangements pale in the face of this fetid mess, surely.

The wife stands behind the counter.

"My friend on the second floor says she's paying sixty dollars for her nice room!" I say, not knowing how else to broach the unfairness of the situation. My hands grip the edge of the ink-stained counter.

"Yes," she says, without expression.

"Well, I'm paying fifty dollars for my mingy cranny!"

I feel hot and a little crazy. Bracey and I are clearly being discriminated against. We have every right to be angry, to snort and whine—not that Bracey shows any inclination in this direction.

"We gave you this room because you brought an animal," she says, not at all kindly. Her eyes turn black, as black as the waves in Penobscot Bay in a January storm.

I begin to shrink under her ferocity.

"But your husband *said* I could bring Bracey . . . "

"Yeah, well, he didn't consult me," she says, shuffling the travel brochures on the counter, arranging Brattleboro, Newfane, and Wilmington in alphabetical order, snapping the thin brochures with colored photographs of steepled churches and covered bridges like cards in a poker game. I imagine her in an eyeshade, shouting at me through the smoke of her cigar: "You mangy animal lover, what do you know about life on our Green Mountain notch with the One-Hundred-Mile View, where pharmaceutical CEOs and Saudi Arabian sheiks luxuriate in pink satin sheets?"

"He's a good dog!" I protest. "Perfectly trained, well behaved—a good deal cleaner than the room you gave us, that's for certain!" I stalk out of the office, my chest pounding.

Wrathful, resentful, I pad back over the wooden walkway to my room. Bracey trots cheerfully behind me over the noisy bent boards. He takes a quick pee on the tire of a Jeep Cherokee, one of the cars packed tightly along the front on the asphalt.

Bracey comes with us in my car when Beth and I drive to a nearby restaurant for supper and then to the Marlboro Festival. I leave the car in the parking lot at the top of the grassy hillside above the music shed.

"I'm going to roll down the windows slightly so you can listen to the music, Bracey," I say, rubbing his chest. Sound travels up the hill from the shed, which is partially open on two sides. "Opera's your thing, I know, but give this a try, too. You might like it.

"You'll hear Felix Galimir, the venerable violinist, play a Mendelssohn string quartet with three young musicians. He's a staying hand, wise and experienced. He spreads his deep expressive powers among the junior players." I stroke Bracey's heavy fur. "I prefer the practice sessions, which we'll attend next week. You can listen to an endless flow of chamber music played by the likes of Richard Goode and other famous musicians." Bracey considers what I say. He's not committed yet. "Also, young players bursting at their seams—all day, every day, on and on. Sublime, bountiful. A week of this, and your ears will pick up the softest bow of a violin, the pianissimist note of a harpsichord." Bracey's ears jiggle.

Beth, looking gorgeously patrician in her long, gauzy dress, and I, in my cotton top and pants, descend the hill in the company of crowds of concertgoers.

After the concert, when we go back to the motel, Bracey rambles over to his Bean bed and watches me prepare for the night. Confident of the routine, he awaits his nighttime biscuits, his invitation to climb on the bed.

"Yes, Bracey, sweetheart, you can sleep on my bed tonight! The hell with the proprietors! We have our rights. Besides, look at that filthy floor! You can't sleep on that!"

His eyes light up as he steps over to my bed, backs up for traction and makes a mighty leap. I offer him his biscuits, which he joyfully eats, scattering crumbs—well, yes—on his own flannel sheet.

Finally, we settle down for the night, and he presses his cold, black nose into my cheek.

⤙ 13 ⤚

JOUSTING

I return to New York in early September for a brief—and possibly final—visit to my apartment, which I've been subletting (illegally) for a couple of years. My most recent renter there has left, and so the apartment is vacant. Am I ready to burn my last bridge to New York? To toss my life of opera, concerts, friends, lovers—well, only the one lately, but perhaps there would have been more had I remained in the city—and eateries: West Side Szechuan, East Side Thai? With my freelancing in Maine continuing apace, it hardly makes sense to hang onto the apartment anymore.

Bracey doesn't accompany me to help with this decision. He's boarding with a friend on Deer Isle. I plug into his old city life without him, though: walk on the bridle path around the Central Park Reservoir and loiter at a distance to observe his former doggie playgroups. No one in my old neighborhood or the park—human or canine—recognizes me without Bracey. I've lost my sassiness, I suppose, and my street smarts. Less of a city person, I walk more slowly, more cautiously, but still cross against the light whenever I get the chance.

If I gave up the apartment, I'd have to dislodge my family antiques. I consider selling them, but a friend, Sandy, a former antiques dealer, does a quick appraisal. Brushing aside her chic, long, prematurely gray hair, she examines each piece carefully.

"The drawer in the French side table doesn't belong to the legs and top. The lowboy is English, not American, because the secondary wood is walnut.

"In a nutshell, what you have here are authentic, nice family pieces. You can never get enough money for them, however. They're more valuable to you if you use them than if you sell them. Several pieces are flawed by later additions that intrude on the originals, dilute their true essence, and hide their fundamental purity," she says, gazing critically at the French table.

"And look at the French marble-top chest; the inlays are falling off! Half of them are gone from the legs."

"I know," I say. "A furniture restorer at the Met Museum looked at it a few years ago and said he could glue on matching inlays at a cost of $5,000, which is as much as the chest would have been *worth* then."

"Keep them," Sandy says, with a wave of her hand at the furniture crowded together in the small apartment. The cars out on Ninety-third Street honk indefatigably.

After she leaves, I stand in the living room, looking around at the desk and tables and chairs. Can I take them all to Maine? Will they fill some unrecognized void in my Maine life? What more could I—or my ghosts—possibly want in that house already filled with family Morris chairs, with rustic, painted tables and bureaus?

I try to imagine Aunt Bessie's Federal mahogany desk in the red room next to the bookcase made out of orange crates: "Oh my God," it will shriek. "What has become of me? What can I possibly say to an orange crate! 'Tell me, my dear, How many fruits did you crate at the zenith of your career?'"

Picture the marble-top and its shedding inlays in the green bedroom with the painted pine bureau: "Cousin Harriet Beecher Stowe wrote on me," the marble-top will wail. "She had literary and moral standards."

Fancy the lowboy in the winter living room near the woodstove: "But how barbarously hot!" it will hiss. My mother always believed robbers wanted to steal it from her house in Wiscasset. In her eighties, ill and occasionally delusional, she walked out onto High Street in her bathrobe one morning at 2 a.m. to warn them off. In time, a friend in a large house across the street gave the lowboy shelter. "I will guard it, Betty," she said. "It will be safe with me." My mother loved her antiques.

I visualize the heavy mahogany sideboard in the big summer living room shouting in retaliation at the slim, French side table with cabriole legs: "We are Arts and Crafts, far more appropriate here than *you*."

The ship models on the mantelpiece halloo to the Connecticut fiddleback maple chairs with rush seats: "Jibe ho! We'll take the wind out of your sails. Belay your sheets, man your winches, hoist your petard!"

"Avast your idle chatter, you French harlots," trumpet the stolid, oak Morris chairs to the foreign assemblage. "You dancehall hostesses, beret-wearing, wine-drinking, Gauloise-puffing French dilettantes!"

I imagine the rooms full of strife: claw feet banging on the boards, brass hardware clanking, pine drawers shuddering open and shut, chairs tipping and rocking on their turned legs. Bracey and I will have to hide in the attic, amidst the smell of bat droppings, pulling up the stairs behind us to exist on bottled water and canned peaches. He'll curl up near an old porcelain washbasin, his nose between his paws, eyes anxious, while I sit on a trunk, listening to the pandemonium beneath us, until the jousting ends. Then, perhaps we'll descend into the quiet: dust and shavings everywhere, the air subdued and light, with forgiveness, compromise, and acceptance shining on each particle. Peace may reign between the plain Americans and the worldly European *mélanges*.

L'histoire de ma vie.

⇥14⇤

MORPHO NIMBUS

"I bought some milkweed in Southwest Harbor this morning," Arlene says, as she walks in the front door of my house on Deer Isle, carrying a large paper bag folded over at the top. I've just returned from my visit to New York, and invited her to stop for lunch.

Her hair, fluffed out against the dark spruces behind the house, cumulus around her head, fills the doorway. Bracey greets her loudly in the small mudroom. His round, cylindrical body wriggles with enthusiasm; he forgets he doesn't miss New York any longer.

Is this a hostess present, I wonder?

"Please show me where I can put the bag," she says, importantly.

Dressed in silky white pants and an abbreviated black tank top, she's the essence of professional New York, this Madison Avenue art director, with gold rings and bracelets gleaming on her fingers, her wrists. We worked on a couple of book projects together several years ago when I was still in New York.

I gesture to the pine chest in the hallway, where she places the bag.

"The milkweed will be all right here," she says.

Ah, so it's not for me.

I serve crabmeat rolls and salad for lunch. She feeds Bracey bits of her roll, allowing him to lick dabs of crabmeat off her fingers. Eyes riveted on her face and hands, body rigidly expectant, his whole world focuses on this temporary, beneficent relationship, waiting for the least or the greatest scrap with equal intensity, a love affair far gone. Sighing, he lays his head on her bare, sandaled feet, satiated, adored and adoring.

Arlene speaks of her heyday on Madison Avenue: jingles for Pepsi Cola and Maxwell House, corporate jets to Panama for photo shoots. Her apartment on Fifth Avenue and house in Kent, Connecticut, however, are for sale. She owes the IRS $200,000 apparently, has further debts of $100,000, and is out of work. I don't ask her what happened. To me, she was always top-of-the-line New York—an altitude, however, that carries its risks.

"I must not forget my milkweed," she says.

"Tell me about it," I say, interested. "Why is it so special?"

"I grow Monarch butterflies in it. The bag is full of feeding caterpillars. The big cluster of milkweed will be totally consumed in a few days," she answers.

"But how do you manage in New York? Where do you track down sufficient milkweed?" I ask.

"Oh, I go to the flower district, to the farmer's markets. I find enough," she says.

"Why do you do it?" I ask.

"I love butterflies. I love making them. I adore watching the caterpillars eat the leaves with their powerful jaws. Sometime, I get up in the night merely to listen to them munch. I enjoy seeing them go into their pupae, into their chrysalides—these metamorphic diurnal insects—before they take the shape of their imago: their final, winged state." She bites into the last of her crabmeat roll.

Bracey, sleeping on her naked feet, stirs, furry images passing through his head, causing him to twitch and snuffle.

"In the end, I've got butterflies flying all around my apartment." She flutters her hands, the rings on her fingers sparkling like the wave caps out on the bay. I recall her sumptuous apartment, with its Biedermeier desk and dining table and chairs, and the Dutch still lifes of pears and cherries and pitchers of cream.

"*Nymphalis antiopa, Cynthia virginiensis, Polygonia interrogationis*—how I adore them! I let them out on my fire escape to fly into the New York noontime sky, up the steeple of the Chrysler Building, the radio/TV tower of the Empire State, the square tops of the World Trade Center." She sips her white wine.

"But what happens to them up among the skyscrapers?" I say.

"Oh, my dear, don't ask. I feel badly." She gazes out the window at the tall spruce and pine. "But they *must* know how beautiful they look among the towers."

She sits up straight suddenly and shakes out her napkin, waking Bracey.

"One morning, when I was taking the elevator to work, a man beside me in the crowded space said, 'I see a butterfly in your hair!' I didn't move—just continued facing forward, staring at the door. And then he said, 'I see another butterfly. My God,' he cried, 'your hair is *full* of butterflies!' The door opened and I walked into my agency's shiny black lacquer lobby, lit by all those recessed lamps up on the ceiling, the butterflies still in my hair, and the man left behind, totally amazed. Or horrified—I have no idea! Anyway, I liked that," she says, pushing at her sumptuous, abundant brown hair.

When the time comes to leave, she opens the bag in the hall. I look inside and see a dozen caterpillars eating the milkweed.

"They'll soon be quiescent," she says, gathering the bag up in her arms.

After she's gone, I clear the dining table and do the dishes. In my oldest jeans with a tear at the right knee and a frayed straw hat of Eleanor's, I go out to the garden and, humming an aria from Mozart's *La Finta Giardiniera*, I find myself imagining her at the corner of Madison Avenue and Fifty-fifth. She's stopping traffic with butterflies floating about her angel's hair, the dusky purple, sunset red, and iridescent lavender shades of the membranous wings lighting up this corner of the city, this New Yorker with the heart of a fashionista naturalist, Amazon explorer in search of insects, adventuress in the jungles of Africa, festooned by canvas bags and butterfly catchers, wearing the order of the Madison Avenue Lepidoptera. Ah, New York, I sigh. I didn't have butterflies in my hair in the sleek, shining offices I trod in the city, but when I allowed them to, my spirits flew aloft into their high ceilings. Now, as I weed the two long rows of Hyper Red Rumple and Lollo Rossa lettuce, I let them soar skyward into the immense blue. Bracey sits dreaming, his eyes half-shut, by the front door among the pots of Trailing Lobelia, Hummingbird Red Nicotiana, and Petite Licorice. I bedeck my straw hat with a garland of Trailing Lobelia: the sapphire regalia heralds my new life.

Back inside, Bracey follows a lost larva as it inches along on five pairs of abdominal legs over the hall rug's hooked tufts, his long, sophisticated nose pressed to the carpet, less than a centimeter behind.

⇥ 15 ⇤

YOU ARE BEAUTIFUL

Early in October, the northwest wind begins to howl through the attic. After removing the family pictures from the wall beneath so they won't fall off, I pull down the attic stairs and climb up into the cold, drafty space. Bracey stays below; the ladder steps are too steep. There's a clutter of antique porcelain washbasins and jugs, old canvas-covered trunks full of faded textiles, and heavy, outmoded suitcases. I wend my way to the vents at each end of the attic and plug them with pink fiberglass insulation I've stored for this purpose.

"Imagine knowing how to insulate vents!" I say proudly to Bracey, who watches me push the stairs back up into the ceiling and replace the photos on the wall. Passing the pictures several times a day in the narrow hall to my bedroom, I hardly ever look at them. They were in my mother's house in Wiscasset. When she died, I brought them here.

In the family vein, the photos are somewhat self-boosterish: my father on the podium with General Smuts at the 1945 San Francisco Conference founding the UN; my parents

Parents greet General Eisenhower
at the Brussels airport

⚹ 185 ⚹

greeting General Eisenhower, sometime in the 1950s, when he was first supreme commander of NATO, at the Brussels airport. Today, however, I suddenly notice the juxtaposition of two photos of my mother and me. My beautiful mother in diaphanous, embroidered silk, holding a feather fan, her wavy dark hair lit from behind, movie-star style. She looks at the viewer directly, with sensuous confidence. In my photo, I'm in my white debutante dress: strapless satin top and tulle skirt, with long white gloves. Straight, brown hair, permed at the ends. The stance is tentative, a bit uncertain; the gaze into the distance dreamy, a little sad. Not bad looking. Good figure.

Was it all a joke when the adult males in my family tossed me about and turned me upside down—"inverted" me, as it were? All done in innocence and with affection, of course, but over many years. Did my father laugh? I was gratified by the attention, but not altogether at ease.

"You have good legs," my father told me.

But I was never called beautiful. That was for my mother and Johnnie, with their classic profiles. Loring and I were second class together.

My brother Johnnie and my mother in Paris

As a child, I remember my mother and Johnnie doing watercolors of rocks on the shore, big pads of rough watercolor paper resting on their laps, as they daintily dabbed pale blues and cool yellows on cream: shapes forming miraculously. My pad was smaller, the paper less textured, less luxuriant, my tin of watercolors childish, my brushes matted, I always thought. The picture I painted dim and indistinct, the sky dark.

"The shadow under that rock needs more burnt umber," my mother said to Johnnie. She pointed her slender paintbrush to the tiny spot in his luminous landscape, the little patch to the right of the sea urchin.

I hear an impatient, guttural sound and look down to see Bracey eyeing me expectantly: it's suppertime. "Sorry, Bracey, dear," I say, following him down the stairs and into the kitchen. "I was lost in a luminous landscape." He leads me directly to the stoneware canister with his kibble on a low shelf near the floor. How satisfying, these little obligations, little rituals. Good for us both.

"Let me have a look at you," my mother said one morning while we waited in her kitchen in Wiscasset for a taxi to take me to the Portland airport and my flight back to New York. "A good last look at you before you go." I stood, dressed for the trip in overcoat and hat, in the doorway between the kitchen and the long hall to the front door. A shaft of light from a window spilled across my mother's drawn face as she sat at the kitchen table. Ill with cancer and angina, she was now in her early eighties. She wore a maroon plaid wool suit and white nylon ruffled blouse. The loss of weight from her illnesses left her looking only more elegant. That morning I'd heard her gag in the bathroom. I didn't know whether to run to help. In the end, I left her alone.

I sat down, and placed my gloves on the table. A Quimper plate with a pretty young Breton peasant woman lay between us. My mother gazed at me for several minutes in silence. She'd never looked at me in such a way before.

"You are beautiful, Bren. I just want to take you all in."

Restless, self-conscious at first, I unbuttoned my coat and slipped off my beret.

"Your hair is stunning," she said.

Not at all used to her admiration, I was suddenly grateful. For loving me. And for being able to say so. The only way she could. I wanted to hold her frailty in my arms. To cry.

The taxi horn sounded on High Street. She rose to put on her charcoal gray loden cape and green hat. Leaning on her mahogany cane with its fox-head handle, she walked me down the path.

"You are beautiful," she repeated.

TOP OF THE STAIRS

"Bring in your petunias," Carol says a few days afterward in October. "Try them inside."

"But I don't have any sun," I say.

"Try anyway," she says, tossing her long, brown hair. "They're a new breed: *Super*tunias." True, they'd bloomed all summer in amazing profusion.

Carol is an artist, a speed-demon genius, not to mention practical—she can plant a whole garden while I dither over a tiny row of nasturtiums.

I transplant a few Supertunias from the garden into two small, cream-colored ceramic flowerboxes and place them on a living room windowsill in my winter part of the house. Lo and behold—they do fine! Petunias! Inside! Light green leaves trail over the sides of the boxes, violet-blue blossoms look out to sea—to mid-autumn's gray bay and smudgy blue islands.

I've lived here for nine years now. Labeled a Year-round Summer Person by islanders, I lead a rich life—far from the city, which, like Bracey, I've grown not to miss. Even the winters no

Looking forward

"Up, up, and away"

longer faze me—in fact, I look forward to them—which is a good thing, since they always seem to come soon . . .

In January, I notice Bracey lying on his side on the kilim in the living room, his legs propped up for support against the side of the sofa— an odd, new position for him. Over the last three months, he's slowed down considerably.

"He has difficulty walking," I say to Dick, my gardener friend, on the phone, "and can't stand for long. His back right leg is almost useless. I'm not sure how much longer he can manage to climb the stairs."

"Sounds like me!" he cries.

"And he can't hear me when I call from behind, unless I yell."

"Yes, yes," he says.

"He caught a terrible virus and was hospitalized for three days. He almost died."

"One can't be careful enough," Dick sagely sympathizes.

I'm talking about Bracey, who is thirteen years old. Dick, of course, is talking about himself.

The conversation repeats itself at parties and in various situations. Friends of my generation seem to identify with my aging dog.

Carol, whose dog died last year, wept steadily for days. "Do you think dogs are sent to us to die before we do so that we'll learn what death is about?" she asks.

Bracey himself is cheerful, doesn't appear to know he has severe leg problems, except when he's confronted with a flight of stairs. He sits at the bottom and whimpers, knowing he won't make it up without a superdog effort.

I urge him on from the top of the stairs each time, my heart in my stomach. What will I do when he can't mount them? Carry him up the long flight? He weighs almost forty pounds now, more than when

We're all of us getting old

we used to waltz. And I've never tried to tote him up the stairs.

"Bracey, you can do it," I call down to him. "Try harder. *Please* try harder!"

I am desperate at the top of the stairs. Fearful of his incapacity, sad to see him age, terrified at the thought of losing him.

We're all of us getting old. I organized a house party for a few friends in mid-October. Reinco called from Brussels. "I've had this virus all summer. Now they think it may be rheumatoid arthritis. My doctor says I mustn't travel."

Blaikie called from New York. "My other leg just went out. They think it's osteoarthritis. I'm in terrible pain. I don't think Bob and I are going to be able to make the trip."

And so there went my house party, planned for a year—my friends halted, like Bracey, on the bottom step.

Bracey needs more time. Despite a thin film over his eyes, they remain fresh; he has pleasures and accomplishments to come. But his problems with the stairs increase. Soon he begins to slip backwards on the pine treads, a puzzled, fretful expression on his face.

"Let's try something else," I say, at last.

I sit on the bottom step and, with Bracey in my lap, one hand supporting him, slowly ascend, tread by tread, on my rear end. "'Up, up and away.'" I sing into his silky, pliant ear. Stirring contentedly in my arms, he rests his cheek against mine. "'Up, up and away. . . . In my beautiful, my beautiful balloon,'" I croon. We do the same thing in reverse coming down. It takes time, but we enjoy the trip.

Bracey also has small lumps I discovered recently under his elbows and on his neck. I'm not alarmed—not yet—but I take him to Dr. Plohr, his vet, who has his practice on Sunshine Road, near the village of Deer Isle. Bracey walks into the clinic sedately. Khristy, a technician, welcomes him fondly: "How's old sugar bun today?"

In the examining room, the boyishly handsome Dr. Plohr runs his expert fingers over Bracey's body. "We'd better do a biopsy and tests," he says. "Why don't you give me an hour or so right now, and I'll call you tomorrow with the results."

"I'd like to see Bracey again today," he says on the phone the next morning. I'm finishing my breakfast of granola and Cheerios at the dining table. Bracey witnesses through the glass front door the crows under the birdfeeder. "Would you bring him in?"

"Oh, no, what's wrong?" I say, my stomach suddenly in knots. "Can't you tell me over the phone?" The kettle on the woodstove begins to whistle shrilly.

"Please just bring him in, if you would. I'll explain when you come."

I kneel down in the front hall next to Bracey, who continues to watch the crows, take his chin in my hand. "Look at me," I say. He wrenches his eyes from the big black birds, who, on spindly, cautious legs, circle a squirrel busily eating seeds tossed down by chickadees. "Bracey, love, we have to see Dr. Plohr again." I hold his gaze for several seconds, then kiss the dark, flecked triangle on his forehead.

"Sweetie pie, you're going to be all right." I know I am, his expression seems to say; but, please, oh, please, let me keep track of those crows.

I zip up my parka and grab a woolly hat and mittens. We walk out into the frosty air to the Subaru, where I help Bracey into the back of the car. The sea beyond us is flat and grizzled.

"Hey, again, handsome fella," Khristy says at the vet's when we arrive. Dr. Plohr lifts Bracey onto his metal examining table. He rubs Bracey's white chest with his large palms.

"I'm afraid I don't have good news for you, Brenda," he says in his soft voice, as he continues to stroke Bracey. "Bracey has lymphoma." He watches me, searching my face with concern.

"My God, what is lymphoma?" I say. "What do you mean by lymphoma?" I lean against the table, suddenly shaking. Dr. Plohr continues to stroke Bracey. I reach toward Bracey, as well, and together Dr. Plohr and I hold his warm, round body. Embraced by the two of us, Bracey remains motionless, his eyes closed.

"What is lymphoma?" I ask again, agonized.

"Cancer of the lymph nodes," Dr. Plohr answers. I start to cry.

"We could try chemotherapy," Dr. Plohr says, "but he's thirteen and a half. He already has back leg problems, and the veins in his legs are going to be hard to find, for treatment."

I bury my face in Bracey's rough winter coat, which smells of ice-cold spruce. "Think it over, what you want to do." He hoists Bracey gently off the table. "There's a good boy," he says softly.

On the way home in the car with Bracey, I cry: big heavy wailing sobs. I can't stop.

As we come down the driveway, it begins to snow: a tiny bit, a few flakes. The house appears to flow into the surrounding spruce and pine, to soften in the woodland with a grace and solemnity I can't help seeing as Japanese.

I park at the foot of the circle, near the front door, and, walking around to the back of the car, I give Bracey a boost down. In the gathering flakes, he shakes himself, sniffs the air, and proceeds to pee over by the rose bushes.

I make a pot of coffee in the kitchen and bring Bracey to a chair by the window in the living room. We watch the crystals whiten the grass and dampen skinny birch branches. This is our house:

Bracey in snow

where our memories are, where our future will take place. He lets out a satisfied sigh, and yawns. I touch the lymph nodes on his neck with my fingertips.

The snow becomes heavier. I almost wish a foot or more would fall and maroon us out on this point, this wonderland—that it would bury us in its cold, cold magic and somehow transform our fate.

"Remember when you were a pup and made corgi angels in the snow?" I say to Bracey. He wriggles in my arms. "Yes, indeedy, that's what you did." I poke him playfully in the ribs. "You'd lie on your *derrière* in the snow and swish back and forth—*et voilà, un ange corgi!*" He smiles and drops his head against my chest. I clasp him closer to me and get another whiff of spruce from his fur.

How long can I maintain this merry guise? I call Sucha, a writer friend, who has two dogs from The Ark, an animal shelter in Cherryfield. I weep over the phone. "Try not to cry in front of him," she says. "He'll worry and eventually figure out why you're crying." I consult with her about chemotherapy. "Well, he'd be scared, for one thing. It would be painful. And the fact is, you're not buying real time," she says. The sun shines palely through a white sliver of sky.

Dr. Plohr and I agree not to try chemo. "Let me know when he stops eating and drinking," he says, "or, you know, when he can't move and the pain is really bad."

"Can you come here when the time comes?" I ask.

"Yes."

The next morning, I bring Bracey with me to a writers' group meeting, held in a winterized summerhouse on the shore. He marches through the front door with his usual confidence: I've been here before, his tail-less rump wags.

The writers surround him, cooing endearments. I'd told them of his condition. "I brought you a special cookie," one says. She bends down and offers him a fragrant peanut butter biscuit. Thin, silver bracelets jingle on her wrist. "Let me hug you," says another, kneeling on the floor to enfold him, her socks red as fire.

I try to write in the long room, in which everyone else is scribbling away in their notebooks—but I want to go home. And so I write over and over and over down the page: "I want to go home."

But what is home, without Bracey? I wonder.

I share every detail of Bracey's life, and he, mine. His ears are always cocked in my direction. The minute I move, his ears quiver: if he can't follow me physically, he follows me in his head—to the kitchen sink, telephone, upstairs.

On our return from the writers' group, I find a message on my answering machine from Judith, an old school friend in New York who has lung cancer: "Oh, the news about Bracey is heartbreaking. I didn't realize that dogs have the same diseases as humans."

Late at night, Bracey and I walk around the exterior of the house and hear the waves pound on the beach. I have my writing, I shout at the dark mass. And I have Bracey. The two things that have made it possible for me to live here on this windy point where the sea roars and the rocks are half the year coated with ice.

At a potluck supper one evening in an old village house in Sunset, friends ask how Bracey is, and I begin to cry. My tears drop onto the crabmeat casserole and broiled scallops, drip into the strawberry mousse. Ginger, a gourmet cook of the first order, takes me by the arm to a quiet corner. "May I cook something special for Bracey? Beef Wellington? Would he like that?"

Suddenly one day, the flooding stops. Two weeks of tears, and without apparent reason, it halts. At lunch in the Harbor Café overlooking the empty port of Stonington, Sucha, who wears her Mexican serape with royal elegance, says in her deep lyrical voice: "Let him go. This is the way it is."

"But I don't *want* him to go," I protest.

"Help him go—otherwise he'll linger to make you happy. Animals sometimes stay too long because people are unable to let go."

"But I can't just watch him die!"

"Try acupuncture for Bracey," Sucha says. "At least, it may make him more comfortable and ease his pain. There's a vet in Bar Harbor, Sandy, who's had huge success with dogs."

So I call Sandy and make an appointment for Bracey to see her in a week.

⇀17⇀

BIS, BIS, BRACEY

"See the horses!" I say to Bracey. We're driving to Bar Harbor—in mid-February—for his first acupuncture appointment with Sandy. I point to three draft horses grazing in a brown field that slopes down to the water. Bracey sits sideways in the back seat and stares down at his paws. He likes riding in the car less and less. He tolerates but doesn't enjoy it.

I view Penobscot and Blue Hill bays—sprinkled with their dozens of islands, harbors, and evergreen forests. Cadillac Mountain, majestic in its coat of snow, appears at every turn, the highest point on the North Atlantic seaboard. It's the grand, majestic presence on this part of the Down East coast.

On Mount Desert Island, everything, compared to Deer Isle, is on a gigantic scale: oceanic rollers, colossal waterscapes, mammoth mansions. The stores and galleries in Bar Harbor are closed for the season. But the barren streets suit me fine right now.

Sandy's acupuncture clinic is located in the veterinary hospital in town. Valerie, a young technician, leads us to the examining room, where she picks up Bracey and places him on the table.

"What a gorgeous pooch," Sandy says, coming into the room. She rubs Bracey's nose fondly, and her hands slide over his lymph nodes. "I think I can help him," she says, and reaches for her needles. Bracey starts to growl and show his teeth, pulling away with all his strength.

"Bracey, for heaven's sake," I say. Mortified, I keep a firm grip on his muzzle. "I'm so sorry!" I say to Sandy. "He's usually such a stoic, but he's already been to the vet twice in the past week or so and had who knows how many needles stuck into him."

"Oh, don't worry. I understand," she says, and runs her fingers through the fur on his chest. Her face is amicable.

"Would you like some sea jerky, Bracey?" Sandy says, pulling a strip out of her breast pocket and offering it to him. He grabs it out of her hand and swallows it. All forgiven now, he gives her his corgi smile. Sandy hands the jerky strips to Valerie to feed him while she proceeds to slip needles into his head, chest, back, and legs. Snatching the jerky in his jaws as fast as he can, Bracey doesn't feel the needles—doesn't even notice them going in, he's so focused. He stands for about fifteen minutes before Sandy takes the needles out.

"Good doggie, Bracey," Sandy says. "You've been a model patient."

Bracey looks expectantly at Valerie and Sandy.

"That's all, sweetheart," Sandy says, lifting him off the table. "No more jerky."

"Bring him again next week, if you like," Sandy says. "The most we can hope for is that the acupuncture will improve his immune system."

"Will it prolong his life?" I ask.

"It will make him *feel* better."

I kiss him on his nose and cheek.

Back home, Bracey barks at the crows under the birdfeeder and chases after them, more slowly now, as they fly away. They chatter at him from high in the birches. "You foolish boy," they call. "You'll never catch us."

In the kitchen, he eats his supper with gusto and licks the leftovers on my plate, too, when I put it on the floor. His spirit seems to have mended.

A week passes and we return to Sandy's clinic. "How's our brave Bracey today?" she says, gliding her hands over him on the examining table. I grip his chest and Valerie feeds him jerky again as Sandy pops needles into him.

We make several more visits to Sandy in the weeks that follow. But the treatment only slows Bracey's decline, and his crippled back legs cause him growing grief. It becomes harder and harder for him to go outside. After a while, he abandons his long walks, preferring simply to lie by the glass door and gaze up the driveway, past the crows and chickadees, into the shadowy forest. He focuses on his pleasures—eating and sleeping—and his primary concern: my whereabouts. Time is simple, but every second counts.

We spend our days together on the sofa, where I write essays on personal wholeness and dancing partners for the writers' group—some of which I read out loud to him—and pay my bills. He sleeps a lot.

By our fifth acupuncture appointment in late March, the needles have started to hurt. Thrashing about, he resists them, especially the ones in his legs. The jerky doesn't help anymore.

I put my arms around his neck and hold him close. "It's okay, Bracey," I murmur. "It's okay." I breathe in his nutty scent and lay my forehead on his nose. In a while, he stops trembling. We gaze at each other. "You're my prince," I say.

After a few minutes, Sandy removes the needles.

"He knows the beef jerky is a cover up," she says, massaging his tummy. "He's caught onto the needles. It's too much of a battle to get them in his legs. I don't think it's going to make sense to bring him back again."

"Of course," I say. I'm not going to cry. Acupuncture was our last hope.

"What symptoms should I be watching for?" I say.

"Well, basically, if he can't get up, he can't go to the bathroom, he can't eat or swallow—that will be the moment."

I can't breathe.

"I don't think I'll be up to it," I manage to say.

"You'll have the strength. You will."

Sandy lifts Bracey off the examining table and we watch him drag his back legs along the carpet to the waiting room.

"What a bewitching dog!" Sandy says as she leans down to say goodbye to him.

I pay the bill at the front desk.

"See you next week," Valerie says.

"I'm afraid not; I think Bracey's all done with acupuncture."

In the car going home, I say to Bracey, "I promised Sucha I wouldn't cry in front of you. And I'm trying not to."

He sits in the back seat, eyes down as usual. I reach behind me to tousle his ruff. "'You're the top!'" I warble. "'You're Mahatma Gandhi./You're the top!/You're Napoleon brandy. . . .'" He relaxes a little and lets out a sigh.

Late that evening, I take him on his last walk of the night. He lies right down in the snow. Lights from the house spread circles in the darkness.

"Please, Bracey. Get up. It's twenty degrees and I'm freezing. I can't stand here forever. You've got to walk. Got to pee."

I'm in my warmest parka, the hood drawn tight over a wool-knit hat.

"It's *windy*, Bracey."

I tramp up and down the driveway, across icy patches and through snow, circling back to Bracey, immobile in the cold. "We can't give *up*," I shout. "It's not the end yet." The trees whip blackly around us.

From his prone position, Bracey licks the snow, slowly, as if it's one great, flattened ice cream cone. He doesn't budge. I half-carry, half-pull him back into the house, where it's warm and bright.

"Time for beddie-byes, Bracey dear," and we bump our way up the stairs as usual: "'Up, up and away. . . .'"

I pile extra flannel sheets under him on my bed as a precaution against any incontinence, and we both manage to sleep a few hours.

The next morning is windless. Through the glass door, I see him pee with his back legs splayed on the ice. He even finds enough traction on the snow to support a bowel movement.

"Bravo!"

My lawyer, Calvin True, has been after me to update my will.

Bis, Bis, Bracey

We've already gone over the details; now I must sign the new will, and Calvin's secretary called a month ago to make an appointment. The day has come.

"Bracey, dear heart, your illness reminds me of my own mortality. It's best I keep this appointment. I'll only be gone a couple of hours. Hold on, big boy."

"My old dog is dying," I say to Calvin as I enter his office in Blue Hill on the mainland. He understands what I'm going through, is duly sympathetic.

Two witnesses, a man and a woman from Calvin's office, enter the conference room. Handed a pen, I sign my Last Will and Testament.

"When the time comes for Bracey, make it a Celebration," people tell me. "It will be an act of love." But what if he isn't sufficiently tranquilized, what if he struggles, will it be like the electric chair? I cannot endure the thought.

The witnesses sign my will, radiating contentment. This is just another workday for them.

"Will you sign a living will, as well?" Calvin asks. He places papers on the table between us. I sign four copies.

Bracey waits at the glass front door.

"I've just made merry with lawyers. Tidied my estate. So the plug can be pulled on me, if need be."

Hauling himself out the door, his back legs collapsed, Bracey draws himself agonizingly slowly to a spot where the sun has taken the snow almost down to the grass, and performs his duties. Spring is finally here, it seems. Maybe he'll be able to keep going at least a while longer.

"Bis, bis, Bracey."

⇀ 18 ↽

LAVENDER BAY

Lying next to Bracey on the floor beside my bed several mornings afterwards, I stroke his white chest. It feels cold to my touch, not at all so slumberously warm as it used to. "'Wake, O wake and sleep no longer,'" I sing into his ear from Bach's *Sleepers Awake* cantata. He stirs and opens his dim eyes slightly.

"Bracey, sweets, I'm going to get my breakfast." Since he takes almost an hour to wake fully, I leave him upstairs. He never tries the stairs by himself now anyway, but waits for me. We go up and down together. Our old routine.

I don't rush my breakfast. The sun blinks dully through pine and fir branches; the bay drowses. Eiders float on the flat sea. As I drink my coffee, I see Wayne and Charlie, who are in the process of putting a new roof on the Trivet, rattle down the driveway in Wayne's truck. I wave at them through the window.

Wayne opens the front door and calls out to me: "We should check the big house for maintenance today, 'fore I work on the Trivet."

"Sure thing—I'll be right out."

It's been less than an hour since I came down. If we do the tour fast, Bracey should be okay.

"The house needs new shingles on the south and east walls," Wayne says, as we stand facing the building a few minutes later.

"I agree," I say quickly.

"And I'm a little worried about that gutter there. Slopes the wrong way," he says. He studies the problem, rubbing his short brown hair with his hand, as robins chirp *cheeriup* in the hawthorn trees and gulls swoop down toward the beach. How long have we been out here? I begin to worry. "Put in a downspout or straighten the gutter?" he ponders.

"Whichever," I say. "You make the decision."

Suddenly, we hear a thump inside the house. "Oh, my God—was that Bracey?" I cry, frozen in alarm. "He hasn't tried to go down the stairs in weeks!" I race indoors, my heart banging. Wayne follows. This can't be happening.

We rush through the hall, stumbling over my gardening boots and outdoor shoes strewn on the floor, to the foot of the stairs. I can hardly bear to look. Bracey lies with his head flat on the carpet, eyes closed, legs splayed. He appears lifeless, but as I fling myself down and put my arms around him, he starts to cry and whimper. "Oh, Bracey, Bracey, my darling, you're alive!" All at once, he flings his head up and arches his back. Whereupon, almost as suddenly, his body becomes rigid. I hang onto him with all my strength. He must be having a seizure. It lasts only a few seconds.

"I never should have left him!" I moan, cradling him.

Wayne bends over and caresses Bracey's nose. "You're going to be okay, old boy," he says. "Listen, it's not your fault, Brenda. He's coming out of it, looks like, huh?" He stays with me a few more minutes until Bracey seems to have recovered somewhat, and subsequently heads off to the Trivet.

Bracey and I remain at the foot of the stairs for about half an hour, his head resting in my lap. I run my hands along the soft fur of his white belly. He yawns and begins to relax. I skim his forehead and nose with my little finger, humming Brünnhilde's magic fire music. Gazing up at me, his eyes flicker.

"Do you want to go pee?" I ask.

He's managed to drag himself in and out of the house these past weeks, never being sorry for himself. With some effort, I carry him outdoors and set him on the frosty grass. He pees lying down, somehow not messing himself. "Good boy, Bracey." A few inches away, he has a bowel movement. A miracle. "Fantastic, love!" Exhausted, but satisfied, he's done his job.

I pick him up to bring him inside. On the doorstep, I feel him stiffen against my chest with another seizure. Frightened, I ease his head onto my shoulder and grasp his round body close. "Hang in there, Bracey darlin'," I murmur into the back of his head, kissing the space between his ears. Gradually, the seizure abates.

I lay him gently on the hall floor. After a few minutes, he struggles to pull himself into the bathroom, where the cool, hard linoleum floor seems to give him relief. He has another seizure. I sit next to him, my back against the small, compact furnace, and lift him into my lap. Knowing the lymph nodes on his neck hurt him, I try to find a more comfortable place for him to rest his head—in the crook of my neck, on my stomach—but nothing will do. The seizure over, we rest, worn out, gazing into each other's eyes, his expression tender, reflective. "You're the best," I whisper.

From my sitting position, I slide him back onto the linoleum and rise to bring his water bowl from the kitchen. I dip my finger in the water and offer it to him to lick. He turns his head away.

Outdoors, chickadees fly to and from the birdfeeder. Bracey's crows walk in stately paces under the feeder.

With a mug of coffee, a blanket and cushions, and my portable phone at hand, I settle on the floor for the day. Bracey closes his eyes and sighs.

"I'm here to stay, love."

I phone Sucha and leave a message. "Bracey has had three seizures this morning," I sob. "I left him upstairs and he fell down them. Shall I call Dr. Plohr, do you think?"

Sucha phones back. "Yes, the time's come. But do *not*, I implore you, Brenda dear, blame yourself for Bracey's fall. Call Dr. Plohr."

I tell Dr. Plohr about Bracey's seizures and not eating or drinking. "I'm so sorry," Dr. Plohr says in his gentlest voice. "As we discussed, I'll come over to your house. This evening, at 6, all right? You'll want to give Bracey ten Diazetam tranquilizers, five milligrams each, two to four hours beforehand, okay? Feed them to him with something he likes to eat. I'll phone the prescription into the pharmacy in Blue Hill immediately."

"Let me drive to Blue Hill for the tranquilizers," Sucha says in her deep, bell-like voice.

"I think *I* need tranquilizers, too!" I tell her, half-laughing, half-weeping. "I'm falling apart."

"Okay, call your doctor, and I'll pick those up for you, as well."

"You're an angel," I say to Sucha from my seat on the bathroom floor when she arrives with the tranquilizers early in the afternoon. She's even found liverwurst for Bracey to take the pills in.

"He's still partly a New York dog, isn't he?" she smiles. "Likes his deli food, don't you, you gorgeous guy?" She reaches down to scratch Bracey lightly under his chin.

Not long after that, Nancy walks through the door with a generous pot of spinach soup.

"Are you ready, dear?" Sucha touches my hand. I fold Bracey against my chest. He opens his eyes, holding my gaze.

"Yes," I say and kiss his paws.

Bending over, Sucha feeds him the tranquilizers, buried in tiny mounds of liverwurst.

"Oh, lord, he's eating! Let's stop this!" I cry. "This is all a horrible mistake!"

"It's only temporary, Brenda," Sucha says calmly. "He's dying; we know that."

I gulp down a tranquilizer with a glass of water, while Sucha and Nancy place chairs in the hall outside the bathroom and talk softly.

Bracey edges himself onto the smooth floor between my legs and lies on his side, head in my lap.

Soon, two other friends arrive. They linger in the hall with Nancy and Sucha, speaking quietly, then enter the bathroom to kneel down beside Bracey. The air is redolent of the women's perfume and the hearty odor of Nancy's spinach soup, warming on the stove in the kitchen. Whiffs of paper-white daffodils planted by Carol in pots by the front door enter the house each time it's opened.

One friend rubs Bracey's stomach. "'Rock a bye baby in the tree-top,'" she slowly sings. The other lightly touches his patrician nose with her fingers. Bracey closes his eyes, breathing more calmly, more slowly, the tranquilizers taking effect.

"Wayne wonders if he could speak with you for a moment in the garden," Sucha says from the bathroom doorway. She takes my place next to Bracey. "Bracey, beautiful Bracey," she lilts, "you are dogdom's king."

"I'd be glad to make a casket for the little fella, if you like," Wayne says, as we stand under the budding birches. "Always had a soft spot for him."

"Oh, my goodness, Wayne, what an incredible offer!"

"Tell me where to dig the grave, and we'll do that, too."

"You're terrific," I say. "Maybe inside the driveway loop? Bracey loves to watch the comings and goings in the driveway, and the crows."

"How about here?" He points to a grassy patch at the foot of the circle, nearest the house. It has a view of the driveway and bird-feeder, but also of the bay and islands, all the way to the Camden Hills. The sun pokes through scattered clouds on its way to the top of Butter Island.

"Perfect," I say.

"Would you mind if I measure the little tike?" he says, with an apologetic dip of his head worthy of a UN diplomat. "Just take a minute."

"Of course, Wayne. How thoughtful."

Wayne follows me back inside to the bathroom. I smooth Bracey's long back while Wayne measures him.

"He may have short legs, but he's not exactly a *small* dog," Wayne says, delicately suspending the tape above Bracey's torso. "Needs a roomy casket."

Bracey lies half asleep, his breathing shallow now. My friends take turns stroking his belly, his ears, his nose. He smells of bay-berry and juniper. "Goodbye, Bracey," they say.

Tranquilized, in a haze, Bracey and I are limply entwined. The furnace throbs at my back.

Nancy hands out bowls of her delectable soup. The hall seems crowded, though there are only four or five people altogether. Wandering in and out of the bathroom, sipping and murmuring to each other, they reach down to pat Bracey's forehead and belly, to fondle his ears. They pat the top of my head, too, and squeeze my arm. "We love you both," they say. "Love you, too," I reply.

"Delicious," Sucha says, as she appreciatively spoons up Nancy's fragrant soup. "Absolutely delicious."

"Hello," Dr. Plohr calls as he opens the glass door at 6 p.m., his lithe, athletic figure outlined against the dimming light. He carries a small bag. "A heartbreaking occasion," he says, nodding to the women with sympathy.

"Would you like a bowl of spinach soup, doctor?" Nancy asks.

"No, thank you," he says, catching sight of Bracey and me in the bathroom.

He walks quickly through the small group and crouches down beside Bracey and me. He presses my arm and brushes Bracey's muzzle with his fingers. "You're a grand boy, Bracey." He starts to open his bag.

"He won't know a thing, Brenda, I promise," he says. "I know this is hard. I think he's ready, if you are. Take your time."

I press my lips to Bracey's head and touch his eyelids. "You're the only one," I whisper through the tears streaming down my face.

In a haze, I watch as Dr. Plohr ties a tourniquet around Bracey's back left leg with his strong hands. I notice his immaculate fingernails as he injects Bracey with another, more powerful sedative. Bracey seems to feel nothing. He falls rapidly asleep, with eyes wide open.

I hold his face in my hands and touch my forehead to his. Slowly, over a period of time, his body relaxes, his breathing hardly noticeable.

Sucha and Nancy stand in the doorway, tears running down

their cheeks. Plohr signals to me with his eyes and injects Bracey a second time. "Goodbye, sweetheart," I breathe into his cheek. Beside me, I hear Dr. Plohr crying. We're all weeping.

"He's gone," Dr. Plohr says finally, his finger held against the side of Bracey's neck.

I clasp Bracey's body to me, stroking the red fur on his back and the white on his chest. I smell his sweet piny odor. Tears fall steadily down my cheeks onto his face.

Dr. Plohr sits with us for a while, then rises effortlessly to his feet. Giving me a faint, consoling smile, he packs his bag and leaves. My friends close the door after him.

Out in the loop, Wayne and Charlie finish digging Bracey's grave. Beside them rests a small, carefully crafted pine casket. Every detail is flawless, including the screws in the lid, waiting to be tightened once the top is in position.

Carrying Bracey's body, which I have wrapped in a clean, white flannel sheet, to the coffin, Wayne slowly lays him in. He fits precisely. I place his collar over him, along with his I.D. tags and favorite toys.

After lowering the coffin into the ground, Wayne and Charlie tactfully leave us. Sucha and our friends, who have followed us out, stand around the burial site. We hold hands in the evening spring light, while Nancy reads stanzas from one of Rilke's *Love Poems to God*:

> God speaks to each of us as he makes us,
> then walks us silently out of the night.
>
> These are the words we dimly hear:
>
> You, sent out beyond your recall,
> go to the limits of your longing.
> Embody me.
>
> Flare up like a flame
> and make big shadows I can move in.
>
> Nearby is the country they call life.
> You will know it by its seriousness.
>
> Give me your hand.

The house casts a long shadow over our little group. Bracey's crows depart to their roosts. The air cools.

When everyone has gone, Wayne and Charlie come back to fill in the hole. "How can I thank you?" I say, watching them shovel the earth back into the ground in the gloaming. It's April, almost warm enough to take the violet-blue Supertunias back out and place them on the shelves flanking the front door. With renewed life and vigor, they will bloom on their high perches—front row balcony seats—and pay their respects to Bracey.

In June, I sit by Bracey's grave, marked by a piece of pink Deer Isle granite and surrounded by low, mugo pines. Ferns bend in the breeze. Birches, leafing out, shift and bow. Eiders moan offshore. Crows go *caw-caw-caw*. The scent of lilac is everywhere.

Anchored in the soil, dressed by honeysuckle vines and spiraea, my house is no longer overbearing, but simple, kindly, and stable. My ghosts' ships sail fulsomely on the mantelpiece. Perhaps I'm one of the family after all, at the helm of the galleon, Eleanor's hand gently laid on mine.

Up the circle of the driveway is the way out. But I think I'll stay awhile, here, close to Bracey's grave, the wind soft on my cheeks, like Bracey's breath, and the house reposeful, and the bay lavender, with patches of blue amidst the dappled waves. A small sail in the distance leans in the wind.

EPILOGUE

A bank of white clouds hides the Camdens. They fill the sky in floating rows, striped red by the setting sun. Pockets of light flash here and there around the bay—over the massive form of Hard Head, then Butter, then Eagle. Sounds of rolling waves surge from the beach.

Standing on my piazza, I gaze at these theatrics in the brisk, late afternoon air. It's fall and I'm still here. Three years later. Without Bracey. But with Bracey's pluck. I move inside to my new bay window, where I'll soon observe the sunset's final minutes. "I can't see the view," I used to say to my grandmother and my aunt in the big, dark living room with its small, mullioned windows. "Go outside," they'd say.

I watch gulls fly north to their roosts, near the causeway, perhaps. Crows noisily join the migration. Cormorants flap their wings on Dunham's Ledge, fully exposed at low tide. Eiders, calling *ah-ooo*, swim northward between the Ledge and shore. Clouds move south.

Hard Head's cliffs flare briefly. Behind the Camdens, the sun descends further yet, leaving a puddle of light on the water off Hard Head. Seaweed glistens on the rocks on my shore. The smell of salt is strong.

The parts of the house Wayne reshingled have by this time weathered gray, like my hair. The new bay window, however, juts out proudly, the wheelhouse on a three-masted schooner. "It will weather, too," I say to my niece and nephews, a little apologetically.

In the seaside gardens, the potentilla still blooms, its small yellow flowers gleaming in the twilight, though Carol and I have

started to put the gardens to bed. We've spread compost, cut back perennials, pulled weeds.

The islands begin to vanish in the haze, to merge with sky and water. I smell seaweed and crab. The eiders stop opposite my house and talk to one another. I think for a moment they must be taking their bearings, reconsidering where to go next. But on they go, decisively.

ACKNOWLEDGMENTS

During the many years it took me to write this memoir, I received immeasurable help from friends, fellow writers, and family members too many to recognize here. I could not have written the book without their generous support. To those named, I extend my thanks first to the readers of one or more complete drafts at various stages of composition: Dan Bailes, Elizabeth Elliott, John O'Brien, Bob and Connie Rosenblum, Blaikie and Bob Worth, and Michael Zuckerman. I am grateful to my friends Suzy Gauthier, Mary Ann Hoberman, Edee Howland, Ginny Paige, Cordy Richards, Eileen Schnurr, and Lee Snow, and the late Philip Harper, who all took the time to read substantial parts of the ms. I salute my neighbors on the Point—Anne Chesney, Sheila Nichols, and the late Mayotta Kendrick—for their thoughtful perusals; and Judy Millon, who not only read the entire ms., but prodded me toward publication. Jane McCloskey lent me her experience as a recent Deer Isle author. Anne-Claude Cotty started me on my bookmaking journey in the largest, esthetic sense of the word and bolstered me along the way.

An enormous debt is owed to the Deer Isle Writers' groups, who presented constructive criticism and steady affirmation throughout the lengthy process of writing this book. With room to list only a few of these dedicated members, I especially note my gratitude to Sucha Cardoza and Nancy Hodermarsky, who went far beyond the call of duty and heroically read the entire, final draft; and to the following who over the years faithfully offered continued, sustained commentary and suggestions: Diane Berlew, Anne Burton, Sandy Cohen, Nancy Dewey, Hendrik Gideonse, D Immonen, Mickey Jacoba, Janet King, Deb Marshall, Jackie Michaud and her husband, Marty Gellert, Judith O'Callaghan, Steve Rifkin, Phil Schirmer, Norma Sheard, Joan Weaver, and Bobbi and Michael Wolf.

I especially appreciate my family, whose close attention and love gave me confidence: my nephew and his wife, Kim and Sue Gilchrist; my niece, Alison Gilchrist; my nephew and his wife, Geoff and Abby Gilchrist; and my late brother, John, who spoke to me of his deep interest in and high expectations for my book during his last weeks. And, of course, Cameron, Ariel, Chelsea, Evan, Noah, and Claire, of whom I am so proud.

Profound thanks are due Susan Hand Shetterly, who guided me with a sensitive, sure hand through several drafts. Linda Winston was instrumental in my finding my extraordinary agent, Rob McQuilkin. Talented and supportive, Rob believed in my book from the start and steered me brilliantly through to completion.

It was a joy to work with Sarah Bauhan, Jane Eklund, and Henry James at Bauhan Publishing. They contributed immense enthusiasm and kind patience to the task of bringing my book to publication.

Heartfelt gratitude to all.

Book design by Sarah Bauhan
Cover design by Henry James